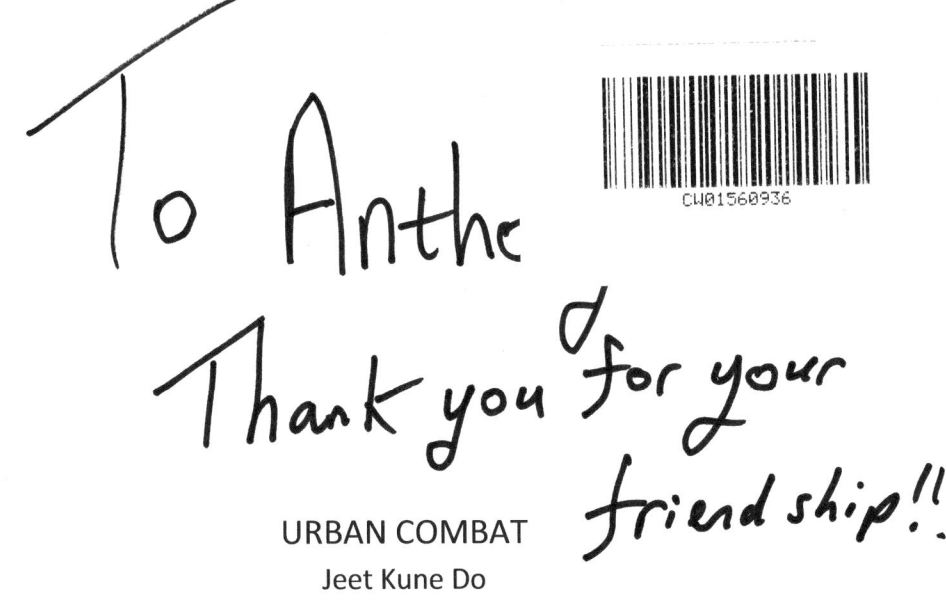

To Anthe

Thank you for your friendship!!

URBAN COMBAT
Jeet Kune Do
by EMIL MARTIROSSIAN

(Technical Kung Fu Editor of Martials Arts Illustrated Magazine UK)

www.emilmartialarts.co.uk

ISBN-13: 978-1466275935

DISCLAIMER

We accept no liability or responsibility for the misuse of the techniques and training methods described in this manual. They are designed for self-preservation only. We do not warrant, condone or in any way suggest the misuse of any of the following material to bring about harm to another person.

This instructional manual is meant as a guide to help people protect themselves and their loved ones only if needed, and as the law agrees is acceptable. Please abide by the law as it applies to you in such circumstances. Furthermore, we do not accept any liability for accidental injury caused by attempting the training methods detailed here.

Consult your doctor before attempting anything explained in this manual. Please be aware that all activity is performed at your own risk.

DEDICATION

I would like to dedicate this book to the memory of my Uncle Armen Martirossian WTF Tae Kwon Do Grand-Master. Also, my brother and Si-gung in Jeet Kune Do Mr Taky Kimura, (Bruce Lee's highest ranked original student and best friend). I would also like to dedicate this book to my God-mother Pheobe Lee for her support and love and for encouraging me to carry on her brother Bruce Lee's legacy here in the UK.

I would also like to dedicate this book to my loving parents Media and Vahik; I would like to thank Small Batch Coffee for all of their support. Plus, I would like to dedicate this book to my nephew William who is just begining his journey through the martial arts and I hope that this book will be of use to him in the future.

Finally, I would like to dedicate this book in honour and loving memory of the legendary 'Sijo Bruce Lee'.

CONTENTS

Above photo: Emil Martirossian and Uncle Armen Martirossian

Above photo: Danny Inosanto, Emil Martirossian and Taky Kimura in Seattle

Above photo: Phoebe Lee and Emil Martirossian in San Francisco

Above photo: Emil Martirossian and Taky Kimura in Seattle
(visting the headstones of Bruce Lee and Brandon Lee).

INTRODUCTION

Bruce Lee's original Jeet Kune Do martial arts system back in the 1970's was a combination of training methods that allows you to be a complete fighter, using unlimited fighting concepts to constantly train your core techniques, mastering all ranges, seeking out the unknown.

Urban Combat is based on the concepts of Jeet Kune Do and also combines other various styles of martial arts resulting in a highly usable realistic modern day self defence system that can be adapted to its user. As a martial artist, I aim to constantly do research and experimentation to discover what fits with the body and a person's abilities during combative mental and physical situations; drawing upon scientific principles, and of course, a transcending philosophy.

There are so many hidden secrets that the old martial arts masters would use to enhance their martial arts way of thinking and in their abilities; some methods have been lost through the years but some are still taught behind closed doors.

The martial arts journey is a very long and lonely road but the path you have chosen is very rewarding in the end. I personally believe that ego has to be kept well away from martial arts. Its not just about punching and kicking someone's face in. In order to be a true martial artist, you need to understand the true spirituality and essence of the art form as well as the technical physical aspects.

Chapter 1
"The Art of Awareness"

"A true warrior tries to avoid fights so that he can live
to fight another day".

We all know that it is best to avoid dark, lonely places. We know that it is smart to stay with friends and not to venture into unfamiliar places by ourselves. However,circumstances can be beyond our control and this is when we find ourselves in danger. Being aware of your surroundings is half the battle, in my experience it is a life saving difference. Knowing what to look for, especially how to read your environment, is of the utmost importance in the game of self protection.

Here, I detail the strategies we utilize in avoiding a conflict before it has a chance to begin. When in doubt, don't try to hide in the shadows. Look at people's faces and try to read what expression they have as they come towards you. Don't make the common mistake of keeping your head down with hands in pockets, for if a surprise attack does happen you will almost certainly not be able to intercept it in this position. If you feel a threat while walking home or someplace, the best thing you can do is simply change your route. This can be applied to anything in life; awareness may be the thing that keeps you alive on the streets.

Keep in mind that an attacker is not always going to come up to you with a frown. He may try to mislead you by smiling first, trapping you for that second. Urban Jeet Kune Do deals in the knowledge that there are 3 zones around everyone, the first 2 constitute your Safety Zone: The distance between yourself and another person that you should consciously aim to protect at all times.

The 3 types of personal space:

The family zone is where you feel most comfortable; reserved only for yourself and very close family. Everyone else is kept away. To measure the family zone, fold your arms and raise them up so that your elbows point outward. Under no circumstances should anyone other than family be allowed past this point. Being aware of this zone is crucial; be weary of anyone who attempts to breach it, give no regard to seemingly friendly intentions. The only exceptions are those you absolutely trust. If you do not know someone well, do not trust them. Protect your family zone and you will protect yourself.

The friend's zone should leave more space, up to the elbow of an outstretched arm. With arms folded and raised again, anyone advancing closer than the tip of the elbow is breaching this zone. Friends should advance to the family zone only after years of trust.

The third zone is for everyone else. It is an arm's reach away, enough for a handshake. It becomes increasingly difficult to defend oneself against an attack that happens at a range closer than your outstretched arm. Do not permit people you do not know and trust past this point. Always trust your inner instincts, and if you feel uncomfortable with the proximity of any person, then move away. Your instincts are usually right.

These days everyone is walking around with mp3 players, mobile phones and the like. There are a lot of distractions out there, when in use they can leave you vulnerable to dangerous situations. Be aware of this every time you decide to drown out the world with your earphones or ignore your surroundings as you incessantly write and send texts on your phone. Avoid using such devices when using public transport, or at least make a compromise i.e. one earphone in with one out, so that you are never completely unaware of your environment. Sight and sound are your most important tools.

Try to keep to areas that you know, especially when you are walking at night. Make a mental note of dark and concealed places and try to avoid them. Also note places of safety; such as open shops, your friend's homes, or a police station, an awareness of such geography is invaluable should you feel you are in danger. Knowing where to go for safety is crucial; being caught in an unfamiliar place without knowing what's where can ruin your chances of escape. Therefore, be mindful of places and routes you have never visited by yourself at night.

Never put yourself in a position where you must walk anything more than a few minutes distance to your home after a night out. If you must walk, go with friends, not by yourself or with someone you just met that night. If you must walk alone, reconsider going out that night altogether. It is simply not worth the risk. Being aware of your surroundings is about more than just avoiding immediate dangers; it is also about avoiding potential future ones.

Planning ahead is an invaluable self- protection tool. Do not ignore its power. Remember that, especially on the street, you should not risk your life. Always have awareness; always look behind you if you ever feel a threat. Gut instinct is a life saver. If you feel that something is wrong, trust yourself. Your body has a natural frequency that can pick up the vibes when there is a violent attack about to take place. We can all tap into this energy. We can all sense violent advances.

People who walk in a confident manner, who seem aware of their surroundings, stand upright and appear relaxed, are far less likely to be attacked than someone who scurries along like a frightened mouse. In short, if you don't appear to be a victim, you are less likely to end up as one. When out and about, walk with confidence and look everyone in their eyes, they are the windows to people's souls. You can tell a lot about someone by their eyes. You can instantly tell if they are going to be a big threat or not. Likewise people can tell a lot about you by yours. Present yourself so that when people do try to read you through your eyes, they see someone who is unafraid and ready. A confident manner is an efficient deterrent to the would-be attacker. Most people planning to hurt you are afraid themselves; show them that you are not.

Urban Jeet Kune Do utilizes the Scale of 1 – 10. My rule of thumb is to never trust a smiling face. When I am approached by a potential attacker, that is anyone I do not know, I am in a danger zone until they pass by or meet and greet me. For ease, mentally scale your situation from 1 – 10. If something seems off, stay alert, be ready, keep them in the third zone, scale the threat at 10. You can still be polite but sum up someone as a 5 or above should you feel suspicious. People you have never met should never be below a 9, people you have met but do not know that well should not pass 5, and close friends can be classed as low as 1. Notice your alert level never falls to 0; this is reserved for family only and even then, it is not good practice to be completely off guard at any time of the day.

If a stranger approaches to ask a question and comes in too close then keep your hands up, palms open and facing forward, protecting your family and friend's zone. This is an important Urban JKD technique known as The Surrender Position. We will delve into its other uses later. Here it is just in case anything happens, because you never know what a stranger's intentions are. It is better to be safe than sorry.

It is unfortunately true that one minute someone will smile, then the next they will stab or shoot you. This is how things are becoming these days, do not expect anyone to care who they hurt or kill. This is the reason why it is very important to know how to defend yourself in uncontrolled situations. Controlled situations are those such as in competitions. I acknowledge that many modern combative sports have few rules and little protection, but rules are still rules, put there for the safety of the competitors; you won't find any on the street. The only arena Urban JKD considers is real life, because that is where the real test is.

When put into a dangerous situation on the street, use whatever available items you have at hand as weapons. Car keys have sharp edges and can be usefully employed to take out someone's eyes. For women, high-heeled shoes can rake down an attacker's shin or stab into their instep (the top of their foot). We won't always be out armed with nunchakus, if ever, but even an umbrella, a pen or some other household object can help you fight if you step in with confidence and employ the element of surprise.

When someone attacks you they probably won't expect you to fight back. That can be your ace in the hole. When attacked, always remain calm and really focus your whole being. Stare at your attacker straight in the eyes and look through him. This will immediately intimidate him. Though avoid this if they are armed, procedures for dealing with armed assailants will be covered in the next chapter. Assert the surrender position, showing that you don't want any trouble, and don't let them into your personal space. Fighting someone outside and inside of your personal space are two different things, the latter you are unlikely to come out of unharmed. This is why we have the 3 zones.

There are many means of protecting your 3 zones, hitting certain pressure points can stop your opponent from advancing any closer. One is to extend the second knuckle down of your middle or forefinger, pushing it into the middle of his chest. Try to practice with a partner to see if he or she can come towards you. They will find that the pain is unbearable; the area is sensitive and full of nerves surrounding the rib cage.

In the street it can be the simplest move that will work. Complicated moves that are very flowery and nice to look at are often useless in a street confrontation and would not last a second. Economy and speed of movement is most important for conserving your energy and catching your attacker off guard.

Remember the golden rules: Be confident. Be direct. Be simple. Be fast. There are exercises that you can do with a sparring partner that will increase your sensitivity and awareness. Sticky-hands/Chi-sao is very useful. Try to practice Chi-sao whilst blindfolded, as this makes it a lot more powerful and dynamic and your hand sensitivity shoots through the roof. Chi-sao is about the sense of touch, if you are relying on your sight you are missing the point and losing the benefit. Also, get your partner to walk around you while you are blindfolded and try to sense where he or she is. This works best outside in the garden or in the park. The more background noise there is to block out the sound of your partner's footsteps the better. The idea is not to hear the footsteps, but to actually sense the whereabouts of the other person.

Trust your gut and ignore your trail of thought. You will not sense someone by thinking about it, so don't. This drill will get you relying on your instincts. Also, working the hubud drill is very good for sensitivity as are using knife drills. When you use the knife (plastic or blunt) for various different drills make sure you don't stop and start. This is all about flowing with the energy. If there are shop windows in the vicinity of where you are walking, use them frequently to check if there's anyone behind you. Don't wear hoods because it blocks your peripheral vision, you may as well be wearing blinkers.

Experiment to find your most effective methods. I personally do Chi-sao, sticky hands and hubud blind folded. This makes your sensitivity far more dynamic and effective. One of the other things I do is to wear very dark sunglasses when I train sensitivity and self defense manoeuvres. After you take of the dark glasses you can see things as clearly as an eagle; in focus and ready.

Another great technique for heightening your sensitivity and general awareness is to put some cotton wool or earplugs in your ears when you train. Again this can be when sparring, for Chi-sao, sticky hands or trapping, etc. This makes your awareness an all round sensation. There are many more training secrets such as these but it is the experimentation and testing to see which ones fit you that matters. These are just the ones that work for me. They may not work for you; it is like trapping and kicking, not everyone can apply trapping or kick to head height, but everyone has their unique attributes. Always try to find the techniques that suit you.

Awareness is a very important subject, especially for street combat, this kind of training will help you with your growth in the martial arts. Sometimes training with the above techniques will make you look and feel silly. Just remember that looking silly and staying alive is better than looking cool and ending up dead. You must ascertain what training works for you and what does not. Never decide before attempting the training however, because if it has worked for someone else it may very well work just as well for you.

Awareness of one's surroundings is the most important thing that I teach my students. In the streets it can be a jungle and you have to have your wits about you. Urban JKD teaches us to be aware but not to show it, because you can't walk down the street frowning and looking dead serious all of the time. You must still enjoy the beauty of life.

The way that I heightened my own awareness skills was purely by investigating some of the old ways that the masters would train hundreds of years ago. They used a lot of mediation and Chi-Gung to exercise the mind. Enhancing your memory also improves awareness. Try memory tricks such as looking at a picture, looking away for a few seconds and then seeing if you can remember what was in the picture. Try going to the supermarket and do your shopping without a list, depend on your memory.

All of your senses should be constantly honed every day to enable you be fully aware of the an environment around you. Don't go through each day as a zombie, looking at the pavement as you walk the street, ignoring the world as it passes by. How can you expect to rely on your ability to be aware of your surroundings when it counts if you spend most of your time shut off from the world? Linger over your food, savoring the taste. Listen to the sounds of nature around you. Enjoy the scent of flowers. Only by becoming well rounded in our feelings will we reach great heights of sensitivity and awareness. These are the secrets of a formidable warrior, the greatest of which are the most in-tuned to their every day lives; they are also at peace the most.

One last point for this chapter, when simply being aware does not prevent a violent attack, when you are forced to react with physical force. The only time you should use your fighting tools is when your back is against the wall, when you have done your best verbally to get out of the situation. Only when non-violent means have failed is it time to show your other side. Pre-emptive striking is a popular course of action these days, but I warn you it is a dangerous one. Be weary of becoming the bad guy, of throwing the first punch when no physical harm has been attempted on you. With good sensitivity training you will never have to throw the first punch in order to win, this is why we train our senses; to see the strike coming, so that we may first intercept and then fight back. With diligent and dedicated training, you'll never have to punch first.

Chapter 2
"Dealing with Confrontation"

"Life on earth was not meant to be an exercise in survival. Life was meant to be a dance between yourself, others and God".

There may be times when you find yourself in trouble, no matter how hard you try to avoid it. For this reason I have devised several strategies, based on years of research that has come directly from my own experiences in real life confrontations. Some years ago, when I was walking home one winter night, I saw two shadows coming towards me. I was scared at that point because I sensed aggressiveness in the people coming towards me. I continued to walk ahead, just to test my instincts, and as the two men flanked me I knew that something would happen. I was very young and they were both much older and bigger. I knew physical defense was my only option. As they passed by my instincts told me to duck, and I did it just as one of the men went to elbow me in the head. He missed and I ran. My instincts saved me and I would like to show you how to use your instincts to save yourselves out there in the real world.

If you are attacked on the street, always remember the Balance Mode: Firstly open your hands (back to the surrender position), stand with both feet parallel, feel for your centre of gravity and assert equal balance throughout your stance, should anything happen your chances of a successful defense are now significantly greater thanks to this simple maneuver. The most important thing to a good defense is balance, if you lose that, everything else crumbles.

Here, a bit of psychology always comes in handy. Making a fist is a sign of aggression on your part, so avoid it, the last thing you want to do is further provoke an attack. Make sure you keep everyone out of your safety zone, it is very important that you have a barrier of space between you and the attacker. Secondly, make sure to look into your opponent's eyes, and do not feel threatened by him. You may still be able to psyche him out at this point. If he is screaming and swearing, this is because he is scared too.

Verbal abuse is his psyching out tool; ask yourself why he is trying to psyche you out. This is because, like you, he doesn't want to take it any further, despite his aggressive demeanor. Remember, as long as you adopt the surrender stance and protect your personal space, you will be in a much better position than your attacker is should neither of you call the other's bluff and the attacker makes the first move.

Sometimes simply talking can be very effective. To engage your attacker in calm conversation may put him off guard and give you time. It can sometimes diffuse the situation altogether, if you direct your comments in a confident and friendly way. And never be tempted to talk down to an attacker, to insult him verbally. No matter how angry his behavior makes you, don't show it. That is adding fuel to the fire.

Sometimes humor, or a smile can help, just be careful not to let your opponent think that you are laughing at him. In a street confrontation anything can happen. This is the street scenario; he could have a few friends with him, so you must keep very alert, and look around carefully to see if there is anyone else around. Just remember that balance is the most important tool. A good solid stance, feet at hips width apart, toes turned slightly inwards. The second most important tool is now your physical defense, only after which should an actual attack on your part follow, but that depends on the situation.

The 3 Modes (BDA):

Balance mode: The surrender position is adopted and a good stable stance is achieved. Key points are keeping calm, relaxing your heart beat, keeping your adrenaline in check, and deep breathing. Do not lose awareness of your surroundings. Do not lose your balance.

Defence mode: Physically defending yourself by intercepting or avoiding the attack altogether. From your balanced position you are protecting your personal space from a physical attack by deflection or other means covered later in this book.

Attack mode: The act of striking back. Notice how we never go to an attack directly from balance. Defence must always precede any attack. There are very few situations where it is necessary to hit first, especially in everyday life. Unless somehow surrounded by 7 guys with knives, there's no need. Attack back if you have to, which your gut instinct will judge appropriately. If an attacker is armed, if there are multiple opponents, or if someone is hell bent on causing you harm, fight back to protect yourself.

Your attackers could have knives, bottles, baseball bats, bricks or even guns, so you must keep your options open. A lot of people in a street situation freeze, but at the end of the day it is your life that is on the line, and you must do everything in your power to make sure you survive the attack.

You could be walking along with your girl/boyfriend when three or four guys start mugging you. At that point things happen really fast, so it is very important that your mind keeps up in these situations. Take a step back, pull your partner aside and keep the attackers away from you as they may be carrying knives or any other weapons. Hold your hands out in front of you, open palms facing out. Whether they kick or punch you should be able to defend it from this position. From here you can reach down to block a kick, or if they throw a haymaker you can block outward with open left hand (easily and quickly done from the surrender position), simultaneously striking the opponent's chin or nose with the palm of the right hand with all your force.

There are several simultaneous blocking/parrying and striking maneuvers I suggest you learn. These are the foundation of Urban JKD, they are simple and effective. Remember, by adopting the surrender position you cut the distance in half and increase the success rate of these techniques. (Please see diagrams on the next pages).

An attacker may try to grab or get you in a head-lock; here your safety zone is in direct danger. It may be breached before you have a chance to stop the advance. To prevent any further damage, aim for simplicity. A direct attack is the key. Grab his family jewels and squeeze hard. Once you do that his head will follow and he will let go. Pain is the best distraction, attacking a sensitive area leaves people open to another attack. Again be direct: elbow the nose, strike the chest, or jab the eyes. Striking sensitive areas cuts your work in half.

Dispatching one or two attackers in such a quick space of time can be enough to deter the others. If three or four people surround you, it doesn't mean you will have to fight them all. If you defend yourself against the first confidently and efficiently, it can be enough to prevent anything further. If there is an interval of time after dispatching your first opponent, warn the rest with your palms facing up, giving them a chance to stop. Only use what you know at the last moment.

Do not be afraid to hurt someone who is attacking you or a loved one. People who try to hurt you have no respect for other people or for themselves. Remember, your personal space is your holy grail. Give no one the right to put it under threat. Defend it with courage and honour. Get into the mindset that your life is the most important thing in your world, if someone is threatening it, if someone is trying to beat you down, hurt you or take sexual advantage of you, you must fight them. Do not be afraid. Tell yourself that this is your personal space; tell yourself that no one is allowed past it, and tell yourself that you will fight anyone who tries.

It is irrelevant how small or weak you think you are; you have just as much right to fight back as anyone else. Do not for a second hide away in the back of your mind and let someone hurt or use you. I am telling you that you are better than that. You can and must protect that which is yours. Because even if you are not successful, at the end of it you will know that you did yourself justice, that you tried your best to protect your honour with courage.

Remember always, criminals don't care, because they would probably only get three or four years if they get caught at all. But you obviously do care, and it is natural in these situations to freeze and become vulnerable. It is my intention to teach you the training and mindset to avoid freezing when it is essential that you act fast and decisively.

Now is the time to make a stand. If someone on a street confronts you in your balance stance, look straight into their eyes, like a hawk or an eagle would. Be focused and ready for any attack. When attacked make sure you begin to breathe deeply. This is very important, as it helps you not to freeze. Focusing on your breathing also prevents you from hyperventilating or panicking, neither of which you need in a crisis situation. Concentrating on your breathing gives you focus, and time to gather your thoughts in an instant to decide your next move. Deep breaths, in and out, and not too quickly, but slowly and regularly, just awaiting the attack. Do not be too eager. Focus on your balance, concentrate on keeping cool and calm, not on what to do and how to do it. Forget about that. You'll never know the answer until you are first attacked, you'll never know what the dance is until the music plays. Don't plan a defense. Your body will know what to do when it happens, but only if you keep it in check beforehand.

Training is the time when we worry about these things, when we question methods and think about the process. Real life is when we let go and just let it happen. That is the secret to a surviving a confrontation. Remember that every attack has a counter attack. You can't go wrong in these situations if you always keep in mind that the most important thing is BDA (Balance, Defence and Attack).

The truth in combat is never be scared of the man with the broken nose or cauliflower ears and missing teeth, be scared of the man who did these things to him. Be more scared of calm people than mad people, mad people are often afraid. Calm people don't need to prove anything.

Urban JKD deals in several unique principles. Some of these we have already covered; such as the 3 zones and the 3 modes (BDA). In the spirit of simplicity, different defensive and attacking manoeuvres are broken down further in terms of directness, efficiency and ease of execution. All have varying levels of complexity and differing rates of success, some more successful than others.

By far the most successful are the techniques known as Offs & Ons. These make up the foundation of Urban JKD's repertoire. They are the techniques that you can always fall back on, they are quite possibly all you may ever need, and they are the most simple. I have prepared some scenarios which demonstrate the off and on movements. These techniques all follow one basic principle, which is the very key to why they are so effective. That is all are made up of two distinct movements: An 'Off' movement, and an 'On' movement (in that order). Off and on techniques are very explosive and will alarm the attacker; you should be able to finish the confrontation with one blow, depending on how you are attacked.

Offs and ons begin and end at the surrender (or ready) position, as should most of your techniques (as this is the unthreatening stance you always want to adopt in a street confrontation). If attacked with a knife, make sure you use the front of your forearms, because if you get cut there you won't bleed to death as the arteries are on the other side. If you have strong, well-conditioned forearms, you can take any blow, even from a baseball bat. Blocking with the forearms is the off movement. The follow-up strike is the on movement.

Remember off and on and you won't go wrong. The off movement can be any type of block, parry or grab. The on movement can be any type of strike that flows directly from the prior off movement, it should be a strike that targets a sensitive area and does not involve any stiff or rigid movements. There should be no discernable pause between the defense and the attack i.e. the off and the on movement. This off and on technique can be applied to various situations. From a straight punch, to a frontal knife thrust, from a knife pointed at your neck, to a hand coming into grab your throat or strike your chest. Slap down the attacking arm with an open palm (off), followed by a reverse-ridge hand chop to the nose (on).

The reverse-ridge hand position mimics a classical karate chop, with thumb tucked in, fingers pointed out and together. The long edge of the hand that runs down the forefinger and the tucked-in thumb is the point of contact. Extend the arm, locking the elbow out. The motion is a swinging one. You step to one side as your attacking hand swings in.

This is perhaps the most powerful hand technique out there. If applied correctly, a followup attack should not be needed.

Never underestimate the power of surprise. An attacker will probably be expecting you to meerly hand over your possessions, and today's wisdom is to do just that, but in my opinion they will hurt you anyway. To me, saying it is better to just give up your wallet or phone to some creep with a knife, than to risk being hurt, is the same as saying it is better to just let someone rape you rather than fight back and risk further abuse; because you cannot rely on the notion that abiding to your attacker's commands will get you out of a situation alive, remember what I spoke of earlier about not trusting a criminal to care for your welfare. If someone has gone through the trouble of putting a knife or gun to your throat, chances are they plan to use it whether you concede to their demands or not.

Don't rely on an attacker to keep you alive. Rely on yourself. Use whatever means necessary to capitalize on that element of surprise. An open hand slap to the temple will knock an attacker out. The trick is to follow through with the blow, to strike as hard as you can. The heel of the hand to the opponent's nose with an upward thrust is deadly. A forceful kick or backhand into the groin will disable someone for enough time for you to escape. Or at least distract the opponent for long enough to apply another attack, such as an eye jab or temple strike. You cannot rely on any one technique, especially a groin strike, to always do the job. Remember the rule of ABC (Attack by Combination). But always be weary of excessiveness. Do what you need to do to ensure that you are safe, nothing more. Because it may only take one strike, and with proper training it mostly does.

If someone attacks you from behind and has their arm around your neck, you must act very quickly. You have only seconds before your air supply is cut off. In this case use whatever means you can to free yourself; an elbow directed behind you to your attacker's body. A high-heeled shoe raked down their shin, a stomp on their instep, a back fist to the groin, fingers thrown overhead and gouged into their eyes, preferably all of these in quick succession (remember ABC). When their grip loosens, break free and face them, if not already on the ground finish the job with a temple strike (swinging open hand). Then make haste home. The swinging motion is important, it triples the effect, meaning even a weaker person can produce immense power.

If your attacker grabs you by the throat from the front, a good finger jab into the eyes should do the trick, followed by a powerful knee strike to the groin. This can then be followed by successive elbows and knees, really the possibilities are endless, and the sky's the limit. But again, keep things simple, only do what you need to do. Anything more and it can work against you.

If, in the worst case scenario, an attacker holds a knife to your neck, you should do the following. This applies particularly if the attacker has an accomplice with him. Go into surrender position, and pretend to beg. Even cry if you have to. You will put him off guard; you will give him nothing to worry about. If you stare into his eyes with your chin up, you're asking for trouble. The knife is there to keep you under control with fear; if you appear threatening he will use it. Do not be in too much of a rush, remember balance first. Now that you have presented yourself as an easy, helpless target, you've got the advantage. Now any kind of attack will be a surprise one.

Nobody expects a blubbering mess who won't look you in the eye to fight back. When the moment presents itself, grab the back of his weapon hand, striking it away from you, at the same time moving your head away from the blade. If the knife is in his right hand you are grabbing with your left first, and vice versa for the other hand. Now grab on with the other hand as well. Your first hand is on the back of his wrist and clasped around it, thumb on back and fingers on wrist. The second cups over this hand and clasps the other side of the attacker's wrist. The tips of your thumbs should either cross-over forming a small X shape or sit side-by-side on the back of his hand, with your fingers reached around his wrist. You are going for control of his wrist, with the knife still in his hand. Twist his wrist rapidly in the other direction, the body should follow the joint, but if he is still standing then apply an explosive kick to his groin, stomach or face. Do not simply throw them down and leave them to get back up, apply a painful arm lock if you can (you can bend his fingers back and break the bone to cause him some damage), or simply strike one of the sensitive areas with your foot and then face the other attacker.

You must flow with your movements and not be stiff. Everything must be done with 100 percent power. In the street you haven't got a chance to say; "Hey let me check my form and see if I can execute a beautiful side kick or a perfect hook punch". Everything happens very fast so you have got to be on the ball. You achieve this by relaxing your body, getting balance first before attempting any defence, and remember to look at where you are going to hit. Don't just go for it in a blind panic, always aim first. Practice your accuracy in class, with enough training you will eventually be able to grab the hand without having to look for it.

Remember, martial arts are great if you are going against someone in competition, but they are not that likely to work against terrorists or people out to kill you. Having a good knowledge of martial arts is not the end of the journey for anyone, it is only the beginning. Out there in the street arena, it is a completely different ball game. Today's martial arts are very limited and watered down. This is the reason I began training in Jeet Kune Do, because it had that sense of being reality based, and I believe that it is the perfect tool for street self defence.

Urban Jeet Kune Do is merely my expression of Jeet Kune Do as a purely self defence based system that is usable in real life attack situations.. It deals with training reflex actions, the real life savers. JKD trapping and punching are very effective in real life encounters; Urban JKD takes these principles and mixes them with a lot of military-based self defence.

You have got to be super fast in the street, because you don't know how many are going to attack you. It could be one or it could be six people. All you have to remember is to have that balance then defence, and if need be attack, but if you attack make sure you don't do it half heartedly and without conviction, because if you do your assailant will be even more angry and aggressive, and come after you even harder.

It is essential to get the job done quickly, one or two seconds if possible. This is why offs and ons are such a big part of the Urban JKD curriculum, they work in real life situations because they can all be executed in 1.2 seconds or less. Always use the simplest technique. Never try to do anything fancy like you see in the movies or you will fall flat on your face. Movie fighting is a completely different story. I stress again that you must work your tools and sharpen everything from your power strikes to your kicks, and work on using your palm rather than your fist.

Palm strikes are a lot more devastating than punching. You will be surprised by how much damage they can cause, and how quickly they can get you out of a street situation. I have found that one of the best forms of training your reflexes is by doing Chi-Sao/sticky hands. Also Bruce Lee's five ways of attack. Once you have mastered these 5, you should be able to experiment with your own; you can have 50 ways of attack if you want. There are countless variations, because there really is no limit in Urban JKD; limits are the last thing you need in a street fight.

The five ways really enhance your awareness, and I think that in many respects Bruce Lee was not only a martial artist who was a hundred years ahead of his time, but that he was tapping into something that was extremely devastating, and I believe that he has developed a complete circle in unarmed combat.

If you really train hard and focus, even before you are attacked you can prevent it from happening. When someone comes towards you, look at the way they are walking towards you and always watch out for out-of-context smiley faces, because that's a cover up. Always keep people that you don't know at arm's length, despite seemingly innocent intentions. I have covered this before in the previous chapter, but it is worth noting again.

If for example, you are standing at the bar in a club, you should still always be aware. If someone comes up at the bar and is looking at you then quickly observe the situation. See if there are any empty bottles around on the bar that he might be able to use against you. Observe how many friends he has got as back up. You have got to be focused. Remember, a focused mind is a positive mind and a positive mind is always a winning mind. If someone taps you on the back when you are in a bar and turns you around with the intention of glassing you in the face, use your forearm and elbow to block it out of the way. With the knife-edge of the same hand strike him under the nose and then strike up under his chin with your palm, sending him off his feet. Then go drink somewhere else.

In the world that we live in now, it is possible that you may even have to face someone armed with a gun. If the gun is pointed at your face at close quarters, use the palms up surrender position again. You can use the same knife defence described earlier, but never get in the way of the barrel. When doing this, move your head away in the opposite direction. If he tries to push the gun back with an outstretched arm the leverage will not allow it to happen. Grab his wrist with your other hand and with both of your hands turn the gun towards him. As you are doing this, deliver a power kick to his stomach. All this has to be done in a blink of an eye. Unless you are fast, the moves will not work and you will be shot. Non-telegraphic movements are invaluable in such circumstances. So always train with them in mind. When attacked or in a fighting situation just move through the fight. In the street you never know what's going to happen; the fight kicks off and you must treat it like a dance, open yourself up to the music.

It is important to train and train as much as possible. Do a lot of reality based training with a partner, and act through scenarios of being attacked by knives, bottles and guns. Drill these moves constantly. Remember that planning and perseverance prevent poor performance. Always plan ahead when you go out of your door, because anything could happen. Hopefully, nothing will ever happen to you but such is life that you never know.

In my own personal experience, the bad things that I have had to undergo all started when I wasn't ready, but luckily I had the necessary training to back me up. However, if you have no training then you'll be in trouble. As I said, it's very important that regardless of age or sex, you must learn the basics and have the knowledge of street self-defence. It may save your life and give you the confidence you need to go forward in life.

Training and preparation gives you a certain energy so that even if there is a confrontation the attacker will be intimidated just because of the way you are holding your posture. Also, when walking, especially in a strange place that you are not familiar with or a dark place, keep to the light. Keep near the road rather than walls or gardens. Be aware of dark shadows or entrances and steer clear of them. Develop eyes in the back of your head. Dedicated training will give you this. Another benefit of constant training is that you will develop the ability to judge when to back off or when to step in. Sometimes attack is the best form of defence.

In the next chapter I will map out some defensive techniques that are fast, explosive and effective. With training, your honed instincts will tell you when to use them.

Chapter 3
"Applying your Tools"

"A willingness to learn without questioning the lesson is essential. How can you question something that is inside of you? Who knows you if you do not know yourself?"

Urban JKD classifies self-defence as the facing of a dangerous situation with both the knowledge and awareness to leave it unharmed. Defence is always far more important than attack, it is defence that will save your life. If attack is needed, make sure it always follows the defence, to ensure that the combat flows along lines dictated by your terms and not your antagonist's.

The on and off methods are the most effective techniques in your arsenal and, if mastered properly, they can get you out of most street confrontations. A very good way to practice the principle of on and off is to use a wooden dummy. It is all well doing your Wing Chun form, but remember that it is a set pattern that someone else invented. You want to try to express yourself and not someone else; otherwise you are following their path and not your own.

It is far better to freestyle on the dummy by using all your tools in a consistently original and spontaneous fashion, aiming for fluidity between movements. Try not to stop and start, but to explode through the movements. This will far better prepare you for the unpredictable world of the street. I encourage you to use your imagination to its fullest potential, visualize the attack and react instantaneously. Apply this concept to your shadow-boxing as well.

When training, do not just concentrate on one aspect! Work on your whole body: hands, forearms, legs, feet, knees, elbows, head, everything should be fine tuned and ready for combat. You can be the best fighter in the world but not when lying on the floor, so always establish your balance before you do anything else. With training you will be able to balance yourself in a very short space of time, and eventually it will become an instinctive movement. This is what you are aiming for, a natural bodily balance. Really train this aspect; hone it, perfect it and you will be able to depend on it when it is essential to your survival.

Try to train for reality based street situations rather than just training to win competitions, because competitions have rules and regulations and the street has no rules at all. In competition, you know that you are not going to get seriously hurt but on the street you cannot expect someone to not try and kill you. Always being aware will cut your chances of being a victim. When you are attacked you have to make sure that your antagonist doesn't get into your personal area, to prevent them from getting to striking distance. Everyone should be kept at arm's length.

Practice avoidance techniques with a partner, moving swiftly and with agility, always on the balls of your feet, swivelling, ducking, bobbing and weaving out of harm's way. Have your partner attack you within a circle, measure the area out to be quite large to begin with, several meters by several meters. As he lunges at you with different punches and kicks, grabs and tackles, anticipate his movements and avoid his attack. Encourage your partner to be creative; attacking you from all ranges, high, middle and low; forcing you to think on your toes. It is very tricky at first, but invaluable training. As you both get better, lessen the area of the circle and incorporate some parries and blocks with your dodging to compensate for the smaller space. Do this until you can successfully avoid blows within a very small space. If you spend long hours dedicated to this type of intensive training, your reaction skills will far exceed normal limits.

When combating an assailant with your bare hands, you must learn to use your head, knees, elbows and feet as well as your hands. The one point to bear in mind when a thug is attacking you is the fact that the thug has but a one-track mind. Strive to keep him off balance, regardless of his size.

Keep moving faster than your opponent and pay absolutely no attention to their size, fierce facial contortions, or their vicious language. Your object is always to attack your opponent at his weakest points, which can be gravitational-based, i.e. throwing him off balance, and applying leverage principles so that his body, and the limbs of his body, are used to work toward his own defeat. "The bigger they are, the harder they fall." It is very important, especially for women or smaller men, to work with this momentum. When facing a much larger, heavier opponent, strength will not cut it. That is when leverage and an assailant's own body weight against them will pay dividends. Especially when targeted at an opponent's naturally weaker joints such as the wrist and fingers.

Please see the following photos over the next pages for a visual example of this.

LONSDALE

LONSDALE
LONDON

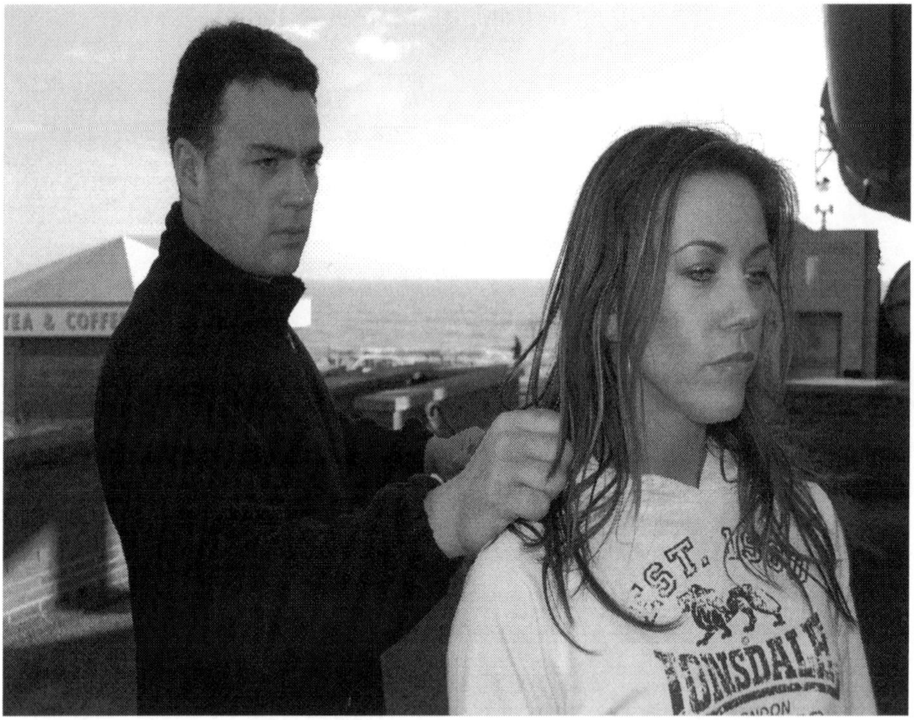

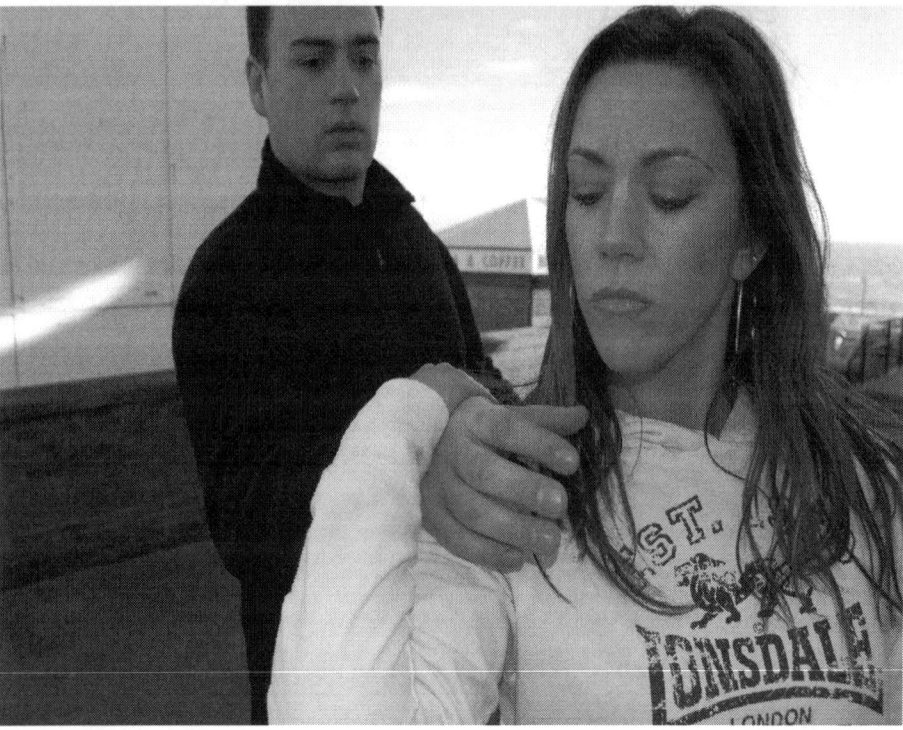

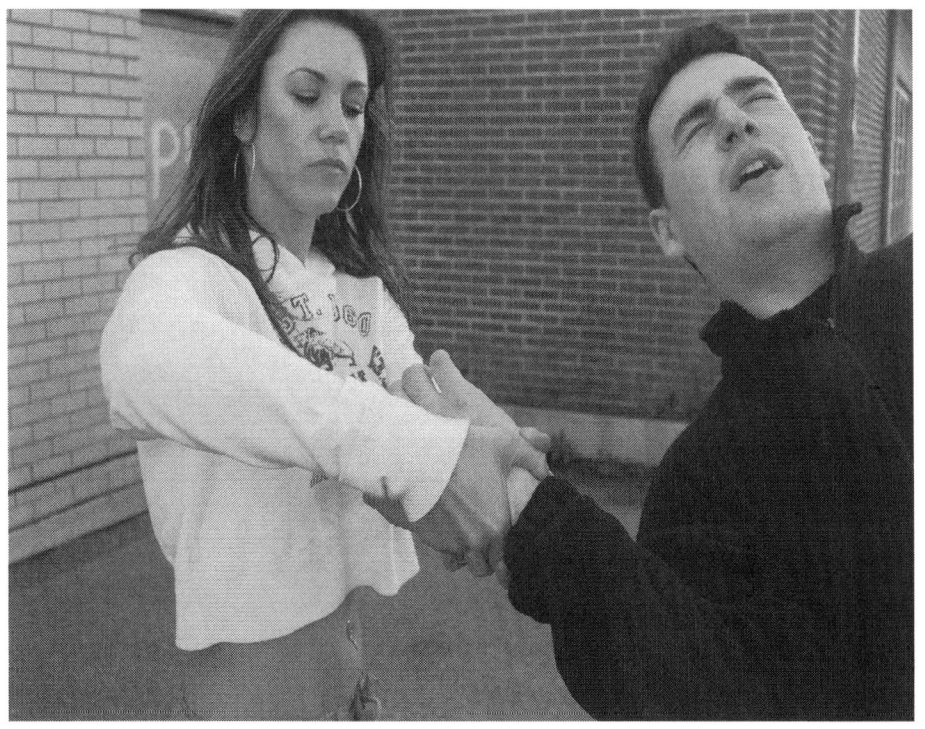

41

When sparring with your partner, practise basic leverage moves over and over again. The Wing Chun based philosophies of weakness against strength are especially useful to practise. Wing Chun is a very good tool for close quarter work, but don't get too caught up in the stance or worry about applying it perfectly. The last thing you are going to check in a street attack is your exact posture; there's no time. You just have to react.

From each Martial Art, take away what works and disregard the unessentials. Don't get caught up in silly techniques, something like: "Oh, if a guy grabs my hand, I'll use the vibrating body technique to make him let go." By the time you have vibrated he's head-butted you, stabbed you or shot you. Don't be a follower of my truth either. Take it on board and make your own truth. Don't be a follower of this or that style; be your own warrior and leave a message behind, so that after you are gone there remains something positive for future generations.

The following three points are of paramount importance when training in any self defence discipline. Always remember them and try to incorporate them into your daily life and routine. These are the things that will help you to apply yourself effectively in a street situation. They are:

1) Awareness – Be cautious and observant of your environment.
2) Preparation – Have a plan beforehand (knowledge of escape routes, etc).
3) Action – The ability to defend yourself instantaneously (the street is unpredictable).

Anything can happen at any time. You can be attacked in a lift, by several people at once, when you answer the doorbell, on public transport, any time. This is why it is essential to train for close-quarters, to get used to not having distance on your side; this is why we work on decreasing the area of the circle. Do not expect to have the luxury of fighting in an area half the size of your training hall.

If several people attack you, take out the one with the biggest mouth first by stepping in quickly and applying a very fast and dynamic figure-four lock, whilst applying your elbow, cracking him in the jaw as you take him down. Remember, that although you have been attacked and your life may be in danger, a true warrior will still maintain that element of compassion for his opponent, so you must be in control of your emotions. If you feel that you have done it and taken him down and he's had enough, let him go; but at the same time do not let compassion work against you, if a deadly weapon is involved, diffuse the threat by any means necessary and leave. You can only be expected to save one life, make it your own.

Remember, you can take the first one out the quickest and always respect that the most dangerous one out of the three may be the one who is saying nothing. You can thrust kick the second one in the lower intestines. Most people think that getting kicked in the balls is painful, but it is unreliable sometimes, whereas a power kick to the lower intestines is far more devastating and destructive.

Take note that, when you knock down the first two, step back and give the final one a chance to back off, whilst enabling you ample time to gather yourself and continue combat. The chances are that everything will be happening very quickly, so make sure that you do give a pause and back off, to give the attacker a chance to leave, and to show them that you are not looking for trouble and you don't want to continue the fight.

Never be in a fighting stance that is too aggressive, this is what makes the surrender position such a useful tool in street defence; it is essentially a double-edged sword. Not only does it cover your safety zone and act to shorten the delivery time of defensive techniques, but it mimics the universal symbol for "I don't want any trouble". It is the sign of surrender after all, the way soldiers tell their enemies that they are unarmed and are no longer a threat. As far as any witnesses are concerned, you are not the antagonist. So if still attacked, whatever ensues on your part is justified.

All fighting is in flow and ebbs. It starts and backs off. Just remember the basics: safety zone, surrender position, balance, defence, attack, off and on. You can never go wrong with them in the street. You have no time to have your hands up and bounce around like you're in a boxing ring. You want to finish it with the most basic tools, that is the key to success. That is the difference between fighting in the ring and having that natural ability to be able to defend yourself in a street confrontation. It doesn't matter how they come at you, be it with knife, bottle or gun. If you have that focus and you have that inner feeling to know how to flow in and out, and to use your explosive power full-on then you'll be okay. But this kind of thing needs a special type of really hardcore training. It is ideal for people employed in security, bodyguards, and air marshals.

Urban JKD is a tool for survival. Reality training should always deal with the simplest techniques that quickly and efficiently solve the situation. Things like a basic palm strike to the solar plexus, or under the chin or nose. These moves should only be used if you know for certain that your life is in danger, as they can be deadly to your opponent. Also, if someone is strangling you, a quick and explosive finger jab into the eyes will make them let go of you. This gives you the chance to give them a full power kick into the groin and run.

When you are in the street, it does not matter how someone confronts you. It could be from the front or the back. If someone tries to grab you from behind, then you can simply head butt the person in the nose with the back of your head. If someone attacks you from behind with his or her arm around your neck, you have only moments before your air supply is cut off, act immediately. A simple gesture of sagging at the knees will fool your attacker into thinking that you have fainted, then you can elbow their ribs or groin, head butt the face and scrape your heel down their shin. Do these things all at once and there is a good chance he will let go. You can even stamp on his toe with full power, you can reach your hand over his head from behind and dig your fingers into his eye sockets, or cup your thumb under his nose and push upwards, hitting nerves that will cause him to back off, leaving you free to turn round and go in for your own attack.

The following visual diagram demonstrates another example of an effective defence against this kind of attack. Remember that your opponent can always try to continue their attack if they spot an opening, always be aware and collected even during your explosive defence so

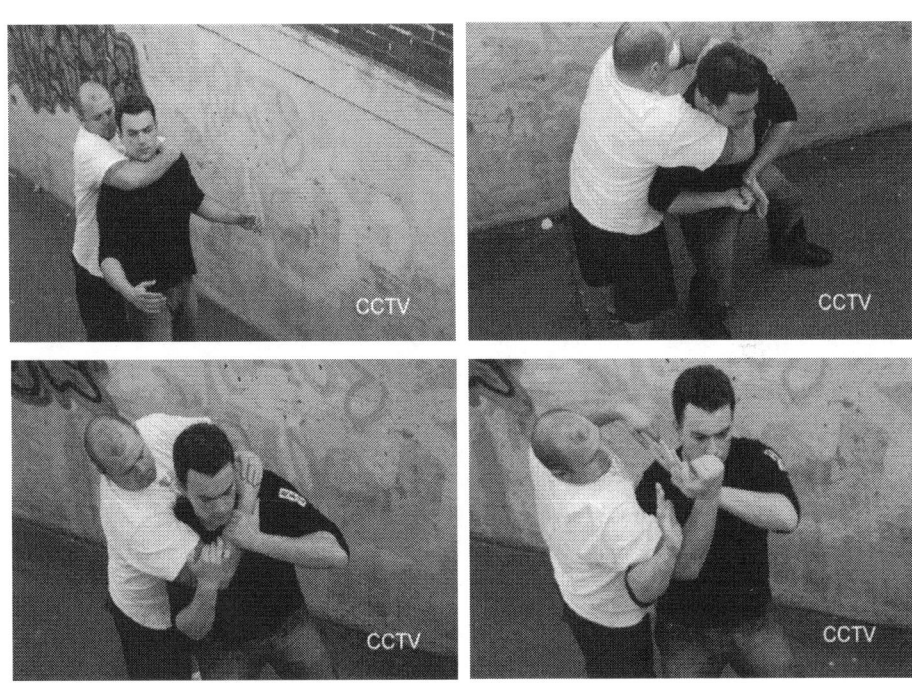

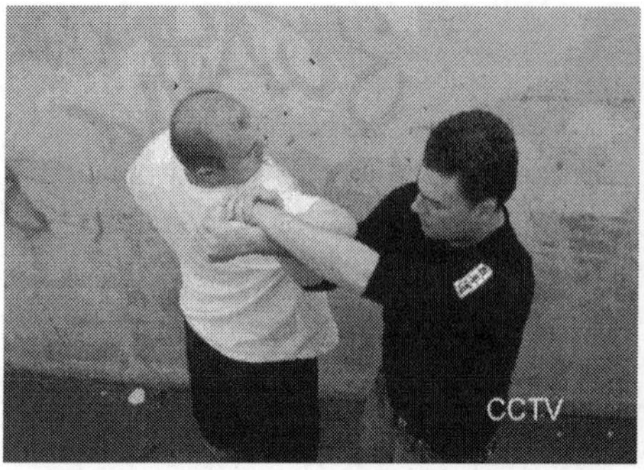
CCTV

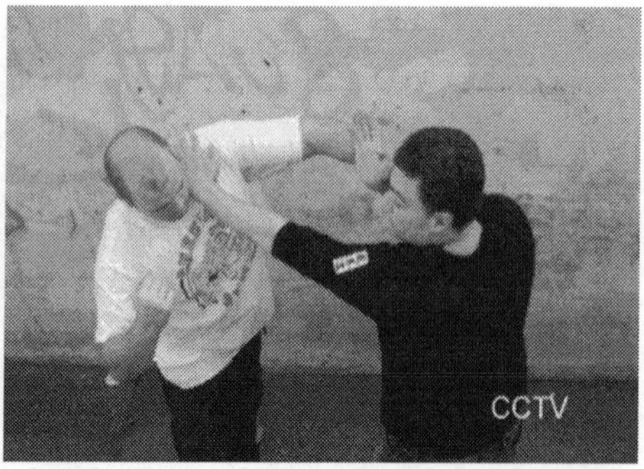
CCTV

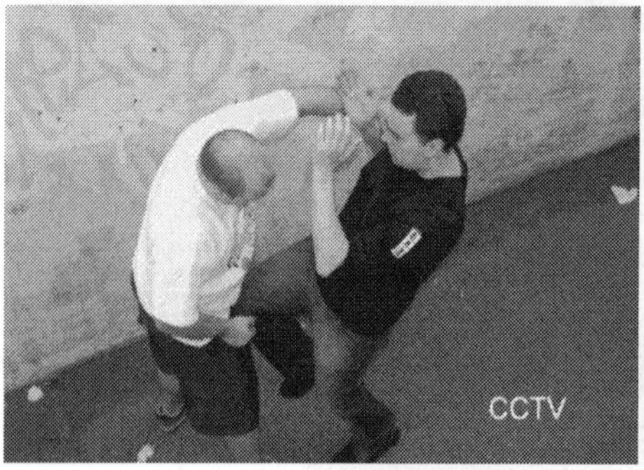
CCTV

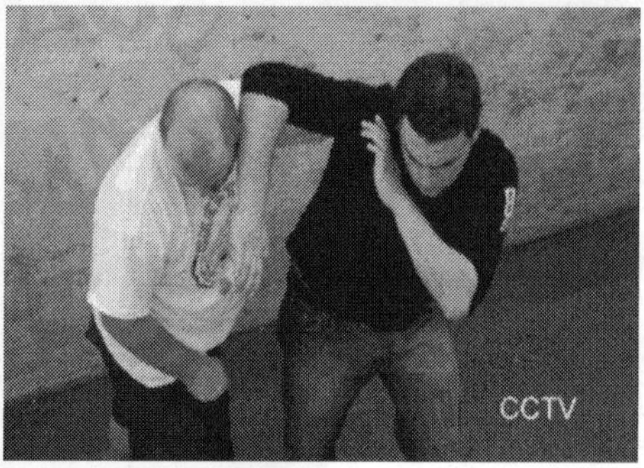
CCTV

CCTV

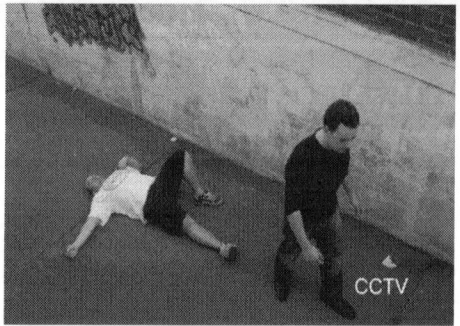

that you can read your opponent's next move and intercept it.
You can see from the diagram that the opponent quickly breaks free
from the arm lock before it is fully applied and throws a hook punch;
this is why we train our bodies to block and strike simultaneously:

The following diagram (below) offers a second example of what to do
when grabbed from behind. This may be easier if you find you are not
strong or confident enough to apply an arm lock. If you can, first stamp
on your attacker's feet to distract him, or even reach behind and grab &
twist his groin, before applying the shown movements. If done right,
this defence can prove devastating!

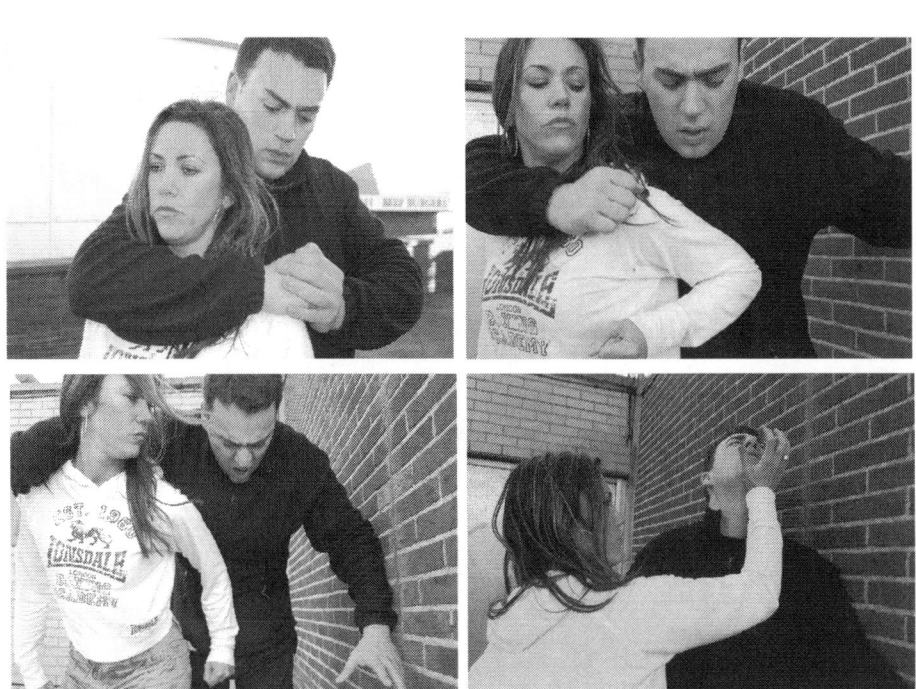

If your attacker grabs you from the front by the throat with one hand, grab hold of it and use your forearm to snap the elbow (see diagram below), followed by a toe kick into the groin, finger jab into the eye, and then run. Depending on the situation, you may need to finger jab the eye first, to first distract him with pain, making it easier to attack his elbow joint if he has not already let go.

If he is still standing and looks like he may recover quickly enough to come after you, a full power slap to the temple may be necessary to ensure your safety. The finger jab, elbow and breaking techniques are devastatingly effective tools and your knowledge of them can be the difference between being a victim and getting aware safely, so try to take them on board and make them your own. These important Urban Combat techniques are demonstrated in the diagram on the previous page.

If someone grabs you with both hands from the front, by the throat or by your collar, you can repeat the same process. But if he gets in close you may have to try something else, use your elbows and knees. If their grip loosens you can grab both of the attacker's hands and trap them (crossing them over one another) before throwing them down. See the diagram below for an example of this very useful technique applied in a real life situation.

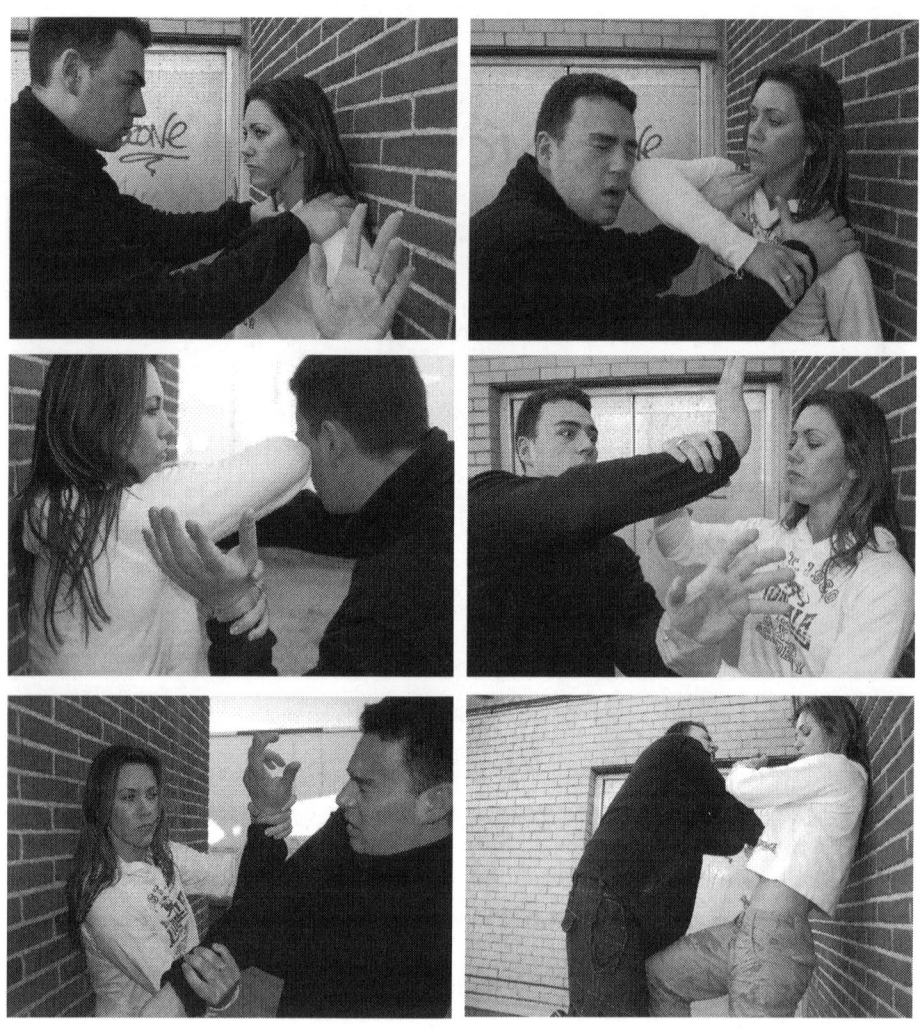

It is essential to note that some attributes you may have naturally, for example speed or power, but even if you don't have them you can train and work hard to get them. Of course it is not easy. It takes a lot of dedication to training. There will be times when you will not be able to avoid an assailant entering your personal space. When that happens, use the advantage of surprise. When he thinks he has gained an advantage, turn it to your advantage. Attack the closest target swiftly. A hard straight punch to the solar plexus or sternum, using the power of your hip behind your body weight or a devastating sidekick or stomp kick to his knee-cap will immobilize him.

I am not against formal martial arts per se. The discipline and training used in most martial arts forms are very beneficial, both physically and mentally, but rigid formality will not help in a street situation. Fancy flying kicks and poses won't save your life, and as for a black belt… well, if you have one you could always slap your opponent on the cheek with it and then try to run away, because it won't do you much else good.

The discipline of martial arts have their place, as long as people take them on board and still do it their way, they can never go wrong. It is a feeling at the end of the day. If you feel that you know what you are doing, then it is right for you and will be effective. The most effective methods are the ones that you make effective, through your own training and experimentation. If you are not willing to experiment, to investigate and to do your own research, but just take on board everything one style or teacher says as the gospel truth of self defence, then you are wasting your time. There is no exact science in self defence; it is far too unpredictable to warrant any one style. The only way that you are ever going to defend yourself properly is if you experiment until you find what works for you, and then train those qualities until the cows come home. It may not be the same for competition, but that is the only way you are going to become efficient in realistic self defence.

Many hand techniques require one to make a fist and it is important that it is done correctly:
(1) The fingers should be curled tightly into the palm.
(2) The thumb curls tightly on top of the fingers.
(3) The fist must be tight, loose fingers can break when hitting an object.

(4) The wrist and fist should be aligned on contact; a bent wrist will certainly break.

Try to avoid hitting the face with a straight knuckle punch:
(a) Fingers and knuckles are very likely to be damaged.
(b) Again, if the wrist is not straight it can twist and break.
In self defence, it is much safer to use a palm strike, back fist or a hammer fist.

For the palm strike:
(5) The palm faces the opponent, hand bent back with fingers curled slightly over.
(6) The strike is with the heel of the palm, the arm straight with the weight of the body behind it. For the back fist, the hand is curled into a normal closed fist striking with the first two knuckles of the back of the hand.

The strike is either:
(7) To the front of the nose if one is to the side of the opponent.
(8) To the top of the nose if one is in front of the opponent.
(9) To the temple (side of the head).

Elbows are very effective for either striking under the jaw, across the face, into the back, the solar plexus or into the groin, e.g. if on the floor. Avoid elbow strikes to the spine or neck unless your life is in mortal danger from an assailant; such blows can cause permanent injury or even death. Never turn your elbows inward, the funny bone lies very close to the elbow joint here and if struck in combat can leave your arm incapacitated.

The legs are very heavy and capable of delivering powerful blows to an opponent. In JKD many powerful kicks are taught from all ranges. The most distinct are the lead leg snapping kicks and the forward burst or burning side kick.

Knees can be very effective for either striking into the solar plexus, the groin or the face. Kneeing the top of someone's thigh is very painful and can put their kicks temporarily out of action.

Try to learn the pressure points on the human body; try to remember at least three spots in different areas. Use these spots and hit your attacker as hard as you can. These spots can be the throat, diaphragm, groin, jaw, kneecap, shin, eyes, and lower ribs. Practice carefully with gentle force on a partner to test effectiveness. Never every strike such areas in training, only ever apply simple pressure, nothing more.

Another valuable tool that not everyone is aware of is your voice. Screaming, shouting, yelling at full capacity can sometimes be enough to scare off an assailant. They don't always want to draw attention to themselves. Some victims are silent with fear... don't be one of them. If nothing else, kick up a fuss. It could help a lot. It could not only frighten off your opponent, it could spur someone into helping you, or at least calling the police. If they are armed, be careful not to infuriate your attackers. If there is a knife or gun at your head, do not make a sound, do not even look up, go into surrender and wait for your moment to strike. Do not wait for them to leave you alive either; you can't rely on that happening.

If you have two or more attackers, never stand in the centre of them, instead try to position yourself where your back is protected from your opponent. Always face your attackers, don't let them get behind you. Remember to concentrate on all of your attackers at the same time. If one attacker gets close, try to attack the other attacker. This attacker will not be expecting to be attacked. This is like a move in chess, try to use all your tools at the proper time. Try to maintain your concentration and be aware of your surroundings. Peripheral vision is an important attribute. Don't let verbal taunts or quick movements distract you. Try not to be nervous. Take deep breaths and be as calm and relaxed as possible.

Don't panic! Believe in your ability to defend yourself and survive. If your attacker seems nervous himself, talk to him and try to make a connection. Find a weak spot and exploit it. Use whatever tactics you can in order to diffuse the situation. I look forgoodness in people; respect and honesty and most important of all, integrity. I know you with one glance. I can see your soul and what you are about. You can't hide from me and it is because of good instructors that I was lucky enough to have trained with, who have taught me the value of this jewel that I now hold in my hand. I am willing to teach the same thing to anyone who can have an open mind and an open heart, to allow the message to flow into their whole being.

Remember that self defence is more than just the act of hurting other people to protect yourself. Defending yourself can be as simple as locking the doors of your car whilst driving, keeping your windows shut at night, or developing your natural tendencies to sense danger, thus avoiding any dangerous situations. It can be learning to defend oneself physically, mentally, emotionally, spiritually, or even verbally. It may be devoted to the needs of other people who depend on you.

Chapter 4
"The Street Arena"

"The truth in combat is within oneself".

A Martial Arts practitioner may train for years, honing his craft and never needing to apply it in a real life situation. These days however, the fact is that people are more likely to meet with extreme situations on the street. You don't necessarily have to be a great fighter to survive in a street situation, but there are certain attributes you will need to acquire. First is a good awareness of your surroundings. Second is confidence; knowing that you are trained to react without freezing or panicking gives great confidence and the way to reach this level is of course by constant and consistent training. It will not come from an on-and-off approach to the martial arts. I have gone into training in great depth in another chapter, suffice to say: read it, do it, and then you will be able to apply it.

In this chaper, I would like to talk about some of the more effective moves and countermoves to apply in a street fight. There are no Queensbury rules here, no politeness and no etiquette. You can fight as dirty as need be in order to save your life and some of the moves I will describe to you are moves that an attacker is unlikely to be prepared for. I have found that JKD has a lot to offer, especially if you are training to defend your life, including the life of your loved ones, in a street attack.

You have to be able to react to any situation without even thinking. Do everything in your power to survive an attack. These days a popular school of thought among many self-defense instructors is to run, and that's fine too, but what if you're not a good runner? Then it's easy enough for your attacker to catch up with you, or if you are out of breath and your assailant gets you on the floor and starts tap dancing on your head, then what?

It is not logical for me just to say to every student "Oh, just run". That might be fine for Olympic runners, but not for all of us. Maybe you find yourself with nowhere to run, how do you intend to run away with a knife against your throat and your back against a wall? In the end running away never solved anything, which is my opinion on the matter. In a street fight you might face multiple attackers, so you must move fast and explosively.

I have found that power slaps work very well. They are effective and do the job when one is attacked. If attacked from behind, you can react effectively without turning around. Direct an elbow behind you with full force, aiming for the attacker's nose, with your arm straight down by your side, a snapping back fist straight into your attacker's groin is another option and should be combined with the elbow to the nose.

A possible sequence of countermoves when bear hugged from behind would be:
1. Thumbs overhead into eyes
2. Elbow to nose (throw several rapid ones if needed)
3. Back fist to groin
Perform these until the assailant releases their grip, then a suitable action would be to:
1. Spin round and power slap the side of the head (repeat right away with other hand on the other side if necessary)
2. Knee/kick to head (if they are bent over)

Should you be bear hugged with your arms trapped as well, execute the following:
1. Throw head backwards (head butt)
2. Stamp on toes (or if wearing high heels, rake down shin)
3. Grab and twist genitals
Once free, perform the same follow-up routine described above.

I remember a friend of mine who was training in Karate for most of his life, a 4th Dan Black belt or higher. Three guys came to the door of the night club where he was working. They were drunk, abusive and they were making rude remarks to the women who were queuing to go in. My friend pushed one of them back and said; "You're not coming in, you're too drunk." The guy pushed him back and my friend jumped in the air and did a perfectly executed flying side kick, just like something out of a movie. The drunk stepped back and my friend landed on his backside. I think he damaged his coccyx very badly too. Anyway, the attackers stamped him to the ground until the other bouncers came and broke it all up. By that time, it was too late and he was hospitalized, but luckily survived the ordeal to tell me. Anecdotes like these abound, but some are worth taking to heart.

As I have said, never attempt anything flashy on the street. The only time this does not apply is when there may be moves that may look flash and yet you know that you could apply them to good effect, then use them. I'm not going to be like the majority of instructors who say "Oh, high kicks don't work, period!" Because that is no different from saying "Oh, I can't apply them properly so ergo they don't work", or JKD instructors who say "Oh, trapping doesn't work because I can't apply it so I'll do the easy thing and put it down instead". Well I'm here to tell you that they all work pretty damn well.

Success in combat depends on two things: Training and your Attitude. If you train in something like mad, and believe you can apply it for yourself with the utmost confidence, it will usually work. Though something's work better than others, and we need to be picky when it comes to what we train specific to street self defense and survival. But we should not underestimate individual differences, if you can't see yourself taking out an attacker with a high kick, even at close range and if the attacker is armed and with others, that doesn't mean someone else isn't up to the task. Look at exponents of Praying Mantis or Hung Gar, if they can apply it in a street situation then it works. I'm more interested in the human style. What is the human form of combat? Again, I have found from my own experience that it's better to stick to the basics: finger jabs, palm strikes, elbows, knees, basic kicks, pressure points, gouging and biting.

You must be wise. Don't get caught up on complex ranges that will only get you in more trouble during the real thing. Just as flashy flying kicks with 520 degree spins should be avoided for your own well being, so to should other things like grappling on the ground. I think it is a great style one-to-one, on a big mat in a big ring. But when the odds are three or four to one, and you are choking-out or arm-barring one of these guys on the ground, you leave yourself completely open to the others who can decide to stab, bottle or stomp on you at any time. The diagram on the next page, highlights effective stand-up evasion and attack maneuvers, including the application of the round kick, bong-sao, back fist, knee and elbow.

1

2

3

4

5

6

7

Grappling, in my own experience, is good for a one-to-one fight and for competitions, but for the street you need something more efficient and to the point. Balance is key; they say that most fights end up on the ground, but to me this reads as most fights are fought by people with poor balance and reactions. If you are quick and explosive you will not end up on the ground. You want to be the one who is left standing and you want your attacker to be on the ground. There are so many moves that defy the imagination. You don't have to buy into the moves you see in the films or the magazines. Most of this is all watered down for the public and there is a lot more to it. Understand that not everything in the dojo will work unless you have:

1. Confidence – to apply what you know and not get caught out by fear
2. Guts - to confront the attacker
3. Belief - in your own ability and that you will not be frightened or hesi-tant

I have constantly tested my tools both in and out of competition. I have found that it is better to experiment when sparring with others, see and test what you have learnt against a resistant opponent. Get your training partner to attack you with a rubber knife, baseball bat or fake gun and see how you would react in that violent situation. Experiment with real knives to test your nerves and desensitize you, but only under the proper supervision of a trained professional.

The Pink Panther movies were pretty funny, but there was some truth in the training techniques of the servant constantly trying to surprise the master and catch him off guard. This is good training. Get your partner to do the same to you whenever possible. Try not to just attack from the front. Do it from the side, back, even kneeling down with your hands behind your back. You need to be able to flow in and out of the fight. Preferably you really want to end the attack in no less than two seconds. Any longer than that increases the chances of you being seriously hurt or even killed. That is why every move must count; every move must be direct and to the point. No fluffing about with drawn out sequences of complicated holds/clinch work that takes forever and removes the element of surprise.

In a street attack you must have your wits about you. You have got to be calm and ready and try not to freak out and lose control of yourself; almost be sleepwalking and try to improvise and let your body do the work. When you are in danger and you need to act, commit to act. Once committed mentally, do it. Don't hesitate. Hesitation can be a very dangerous thing. Don't think in this kind of situation but feel. Feel everything that is around you. Is there more than one person? Do they have weapons; bottles, knifes etc. A street fighter is completely different to a professional martial artist. A martial artist knows various techniques, yet a very experienced street fighter will be cunning as a fox and will know how to get in and out. He will also be able to take and absorb shots to the body and face because he is conditioned for the street arena, whereas the martial artist can know thousands of techniques but not be fully conditioned.

I stress again street fighting is completely different to competition fighting. Competition fighting doesn't even come close to real life scenarios. Don't forget that there are no rules of etiquette when you are fighting for your survival. Use whatever dirty tricks you need to win:

- Footwork.
- Mobility.
- Power Kicking.
- Punching.

These are the tools that I suggest need to be sharpened for street fighting. Mobility is very important; a good fighter will finish the job while standing, he won't take the fight to the floor. When you get attacked remember that adrenaline is a poison. Too much of it will kill you but usually it lasts for about 30 seconds and that is how long you have to survive the attack and move on.

Remember always, when in a street fighting mode, to use ABC: attack by combination,or...

A -Assimilate
B - Begin
C - Carry out

The most important factor is that you must be fluid and alert at all times and ready for whatever comes, especially in the street anything goes so you must have all your tools sharpened even to a point where you are paranoid about who comes close to you. To learn how to fight one's enemy without the expense of one's own life is the ultimate goal.

Real street fighters have the alert eyes of an eagle, the cunning mind of a fox, a cat's swift reactions and the fierceness & toughness of a leopard. They also possess the promptness of a cobra and the patience of a camel. He who obtains all these advantages will be the perfect Urban Combat practitioner. The strategy of fighting is not just physical but is mainly controlled by our brain. In this case our brain is like a computer and we must feed it as much information as possible before the computer can give a satisfactory answer. Study and take note of the trap and strike maneuver, as well as the figure-four lock, demonstrated in the following diagrams (also notice how you can sneak in an elbow strike when applying the figure-four lock):

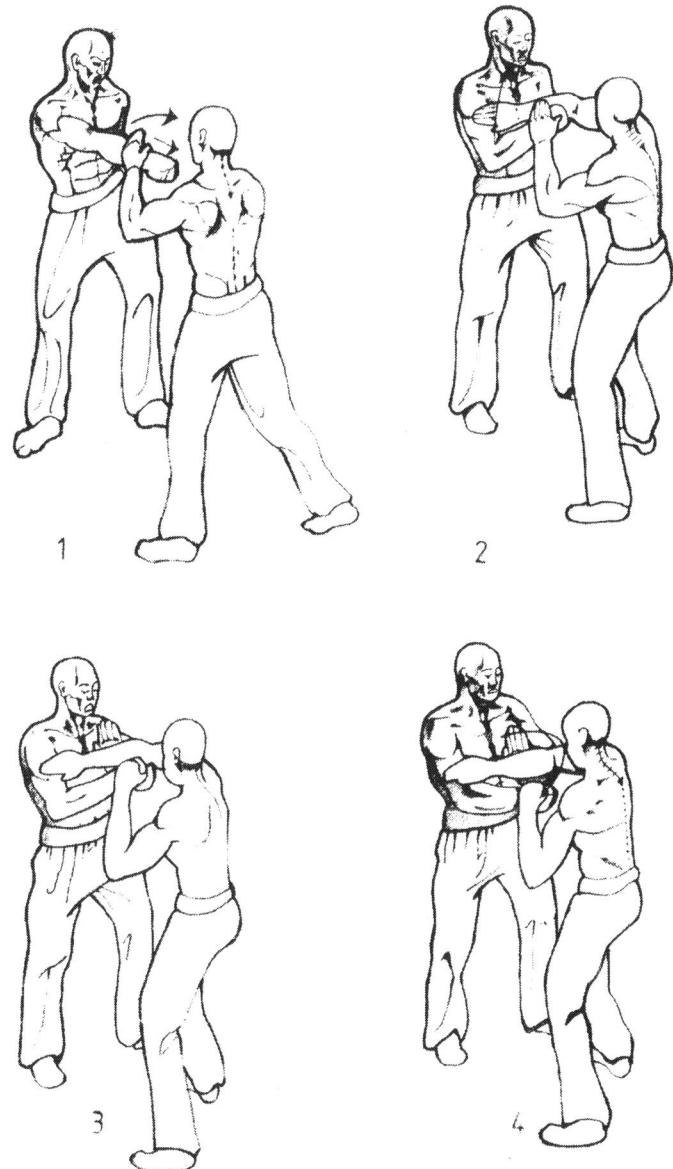

1

2

3

4

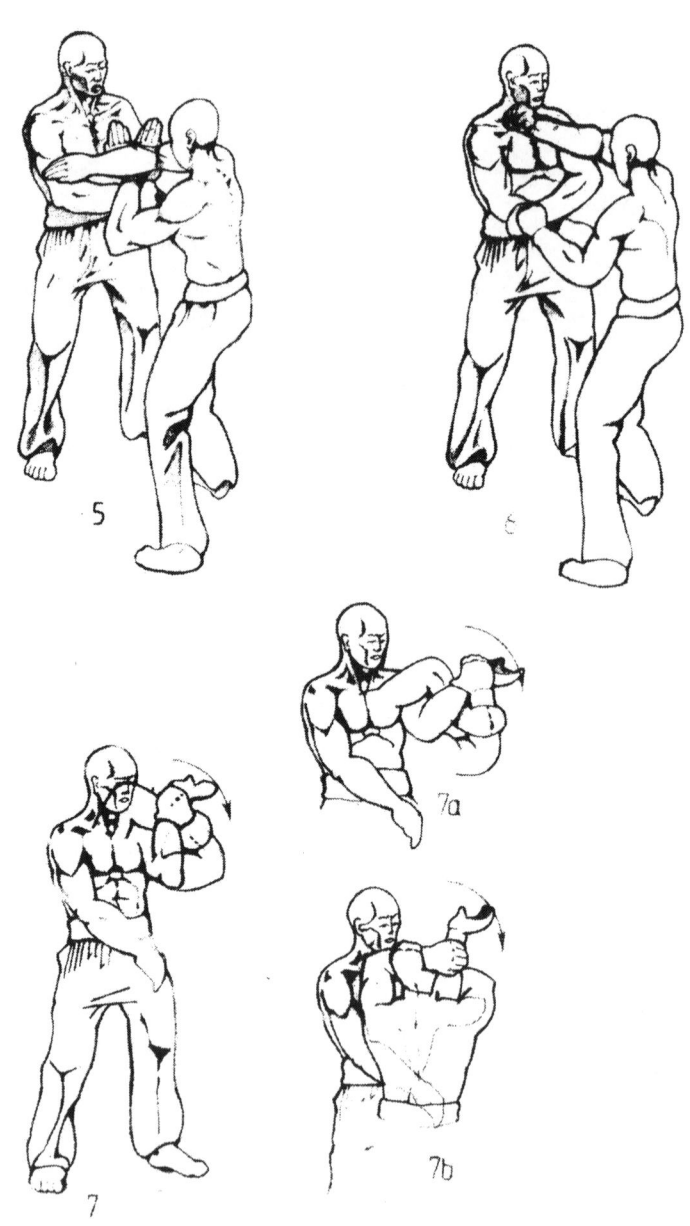

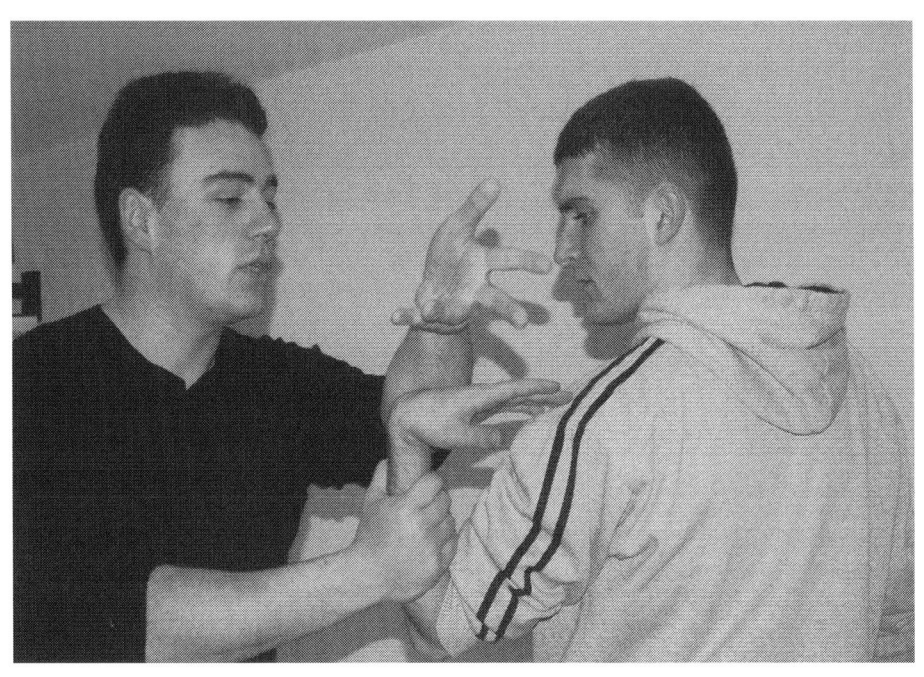

At the end of the day, my methods are concerned mainly with fighting but at the same time it teaches you to find and ultimately use your own way. There's nothing wrong with any art if you can use it to defend yourself, whether you study Judo, Karate, Wing Chun or whatever, as long as you can get out of a life or death situation then what's to complain about? You should study and make the arts work for you and find your own way of expressing them, not just the founder's way.

There is no substitute for hard training, you can either hack it or not waste your time. I'm not here to teach you Mickey Mouse techniques. This goes beyond technique; it is about tapping into the energy and using the energy to flow in and out. It has got to just happen; you don't hit or trap with conscious intent, your body does it automatically. I'm not responsible for what is happening inside me, my body and mind are. If you look carefully you will see that everyone in the universe is on his or her own personal journey and it is fascinating when you put the puzzle together and see how it truly works.

To lock oneself up in one's own world is robbing oneself of the real meaning of martial arts. My Urban Combat possesses a horrible power of destruction with a series of the techniques that, much like flowing water, cannot be stopped. It's not for competition and all my defense practices are done standing up. You have no time to take a fight to the ground nor does my form have grappling because in a real situation there is no time for that. Our groundwork ends on the way to the ground, There will be no time to put someone in arm bar in a life and death situation.

People can argue that you should train everything in order to be prepared for all circumstances, of course this is true, and I admit I have preached this myself. I have trained grappling vigorously, but to the point where I have recognized its limits. I am now at the stage where my training is focused 100% on keeping myself from being taken down, I no longer consider being on the floor.

I think that all street self defence practitioners should be aiming to reach this stage: where you are focused on defending yourself while not being taken to the ground, rather than on what to do once you're there.

Urban Combat aims for strength, speed and accuracy. It stresses the training of free combat and my method is very practical, but again to understand it you must have the right mind and be able to read the opponent. Not only in a fight situation, but you should be able to look into someone's eyes and see their soul. I have seen in the past things that I did not like but I have kept my mouth shut because I know what character someone possesses and if they have what it takes and I have always been right. Once you know yourself you know others.

Urban Combat is all about feeling; that's how you survive in a street confrontation. If you feel that someone is following you then you cross the road. If you are walking down the street and someone is coming towards you then you sense if that person is okay. You can usually pick it up with the way they are, and it is not always the big guy with his arms out who is a threat. Remember looks can deceive. In a scenario where you are walking down the street minding your own business and you spot a gang of five or six people and they are loud and are smashing things and yelling and swearing, then the best defense for that situation is don't even bother walking that way; go the other way. If you have bumped into them by yourself then that's another story, then the most important factor is balance; arms up palms facing forward in surrender position.

Never make a pre-emptive strike, always remain in balance mode. The Urban Combat practitioner never starts the attack. Our job is to defend ourselves and our loved ones. Certain techniques that you can apply; these are called dirty tricks just in case you want to escape quickly and safely:

1. When attacked have your balance mode, palms facing forward, and go forward with your hands up and start moving them up and down, up and down, until finally the attacker will look at your hands and there's the opportunity to strike the groin with a front kick very quickly and efficiently. This should bring him to the ground and you can make a quick escape.

2. When the opponent is swearing and is being very threatening towards you and he goes to strike, you must bob and weave, then say to

him you don't want trouble and make him think you are scared of him. Offer him your hand and see if he will shake it and if he reaches out for your hand (in a threatening manner) or you have the opportunity to grab it otherwise then hold it very tightly and pull him forward, following immediately with an elbow strike into his jaw, then run.

3. If he reaches out to stab you, use an off and on technique then grab his groin from behind his back and lift him off the floor taking him head first in to the ground and then run.

Maybe you are walking out of a disco club with your boy/girlfriend, when three guys approach you and you notice that one has a bottle and the other is reaching for something in his coat. Immediately throw your keys towards the guy with the bottle in his hand then jump in with a front kick to his groin as you do this. The other guy pulls out a knife so be in on-guard position. The other opponent will probably be egging him on to stab you and as he lunges forward, use a quick explosive Bong-Sao from Wing Chun followed up with an explosive back-fist in to his nose, then do the figure-four lock and take him down, but remember, don't hold him down or try and grapple him as you have one more attacker left. Again have your palms facing forward in surrender position say to him that you don't want any trouble and you don't want to hurt him. He will probably be calling you every name under the sun but don't worry; the ball is in your court. If he runs off that's fine, don't bother chasing him but if he's stupid enough to start find the most straightforward way of putting him down. If he goes for a wild hook punch block with your left hand at the same time sending out a finger jab into his eyes then step in and lock his hand and take him down and hold him until the police arrive.

The diagram on the next page demonstrates another effective defence if attacked in a club, making use of the bong-sao, knife-hand chop, round kick, and elbow. For those who are not comfortable kicking high, substitute a power slap to the side of the head or the nose instead. I stress in this day and age that you don't want to be worrying about the next belt or grading, you just want to learn something that works quickly and effectively for survival in the street arena because anything goes out there. The street is a jungle and you must be like a tiger who keeps quiet and doesn't cause harm to anyone but if someone tries to harm your family or loved ones that's when the animal should come out from within.

These are just few examples of the techniques that are used in Urban Combat, there are at least a hundred dirty tricks using anything really from newspapers to pens. They say that the pen is mightier than the sword and sometimes I take this literally. You can even use your belt if it has a buckle on the end. If you get attacked by, say, four or five guys it's a great tool for defending your personal space. Test these things first though, see if they work for you, no good doing it on the day and ending up with your trousers round your ankles!

Remember that you have no armour. Keep your guard up at all times. Use your hands to protect your face, the outside of your forearms to protect the delicate inner sides. Your toes slightly turned in to protect your groin. Attach without defense is useless and will not save your life. In Urban Combat we train for years until everything comes full circle, the more complex things become, the simpler we realize things are. No matter how complex, the principle is always simple; it always comes back to BDA (balance, defence and attack).

Chapter 5
"Training your Tools"

"Great soldiers aren't born, they're built".

I believe my expression of JKD works because all its components compliment one another, with an emphasis on the principle that 'anything goes'; hence being highly suited to an urban environment. You can use Urban JKD in any situation because all tools are incorporated, such as: punching, kicking, trapping, gouging, biting or whatever else is called for in the situation. It is fast, effective and explosive, but it takes dedication and training to be ready for the real thing.

What I teach is user friendly for everyone; men, women or children. Anyone can adapt it to suit one's particular strengths and weaknesses. As in any discipline, it is the preparation that makes all the difference. Training prepares your body for that time when you need it to react. There are no short-cuts or easy ways around this. The more you train, the better your reaction times, and the safer you will be in the world arena.

If you are someone who exercises regularly, then starting on my training regime will not be too difficult for you, but if you are a stranger to the gym, then build up slowly. Always make sure before starting any new training schedules that your health is good, and that your doctor approves of you performing these workouts. It is useful to know that, during training, you don't need to use very heavy weights. Try to use natural elements, such as your own body's force and weight. Heavy weights are good, they will build your muscles and power, but too bulky a stature can slow you down.

A body builder does not move as fast or as fluidly as a proper martial artist should. Many repetitions of fluid movements with lighter weights will give you better results than trying to strain and heft great heavy weights in an attempt to look macho. But do not fall for the myth that lifting heavy weights will suddenly turn you into a Mr. Universe look-alike over a mere few months. Unless you train for 5+ hours a day for 5 years with big weights and munch on muscle enhancing drugs then you're in no danger. You want to use heavy weights that your body can handle without unnecessary strain, because a bigger muscle is a stronger one, but too big a muscle is no good outside of a posing contest.

When you look at pictures of Bruce Lee's physique, these will give you an idea of what you should be aiming for. Your goal should be to be lean, explosive and powerful. I always recommend using a lot of isometric exercises, as they really help with muscle memory. Training should be catered to the individual, not the individual to the training. Training will always be the most important factor in learning any form of self-defence. You need to be in top form and ready for anything, because in the street arena anything can happen. You must hone your tools to a very high level. A gym is not always necessary, there are many natural tools found in the outside world which we can use to condition our bodies, see the diagram on the next page for just one method I use, the emphasis being on conditioning the hands and overall body.

It is not just physical training that is important. You must also train your mind to become in-tune with everything around you, so that eventually you can sense danger before you even see it. There are various different things that you can do to enhance your mind power. One of the things I find useful is meditation, which I cover fully in the last chapter, because it teaches your mind to not be so easily distracted.

Tai Chi and Yoga are also very useful additions to training schedules. If it is practical for you to learn a little, or a lot of both these disciplines, they will give you great benefits as an all round warrior. Tai Chi will ground you and build up core strength and inner energy. Yoga will improve your flexibility, therefore helping to avoid injuries when you are training. Both Tai Chi and Yoga help enormously with balance, and good balance is essential in combat. Good balance can mean the difference between staying safe on your feet or being in a dangerous position, flat on your back on the ground.

Before any exercise regime it is imperative to stretch. Stretching will benefit you in many ways. The main aspect being avoidance of injury when you train and fight. It also helps your flexibility and balance and adds dynamism to your punches and kicks. Start with the side splits. You will find that daily practice will help you get lower and lower. Then try to do side stretches, front stretch, back stretch and leg raises against a high bar. They key is to breathe deeply and to take your sweet time, the slower and more gentle you move the better. Hold stretches for at least 30 seconds. Stretch both sides of your body equally. Stretch again at the end of any exercise session to cool down. As you become more flexible you will be able to take a lot more.

The serious martial artist with years of disciplined stretching will be able to push his body to the limits. I remember spending up to an hour at a time in a full side split as my flexibility progressed. It requires daily dedication and years of patience, the benefits are more than worthwhile however. To start, 10 – 15 minutes a day is more than enough. Be consistent and patient and results will come. This is the easiest part of your training so enjoy it, stretching can be a very relaxing experience; it will benefit a stress-free life.

Time is no excuse, instead of sitting in front of the telly, go into splits, while sitting at your computer, stretch your neck or slowly rotate your feet in circles. For some of the stretches I use and recommend, see the following diagram on the next page.

We all need to find our own path, and every training session should be designed to fit your own physical abilities. Don't bother learning how to do fancy somersaults or back flips. These tricks will not get you anywhere in reality, particularly if there is a hard core gang on your tail. It is much better to train realistically. When training I recommend that you focus most on these three points:

1) Speed
2) Strength
3) Energy

When training, you must promote your ability, and also explore your weaknesses. The reason for this is self-evident really. If you only work on your good points, the sculpture that you are trying to create within yourself will never be complete. Can you kick as well as you can punch? Can you trap as well as you can grapple? Is your left side as good as your right side, or vice versa? Speed is always of the essence. The more rapid your moves, the faster you will dispatch your enemies. The best way to test your speed is to have a training partner stand in front of you and then strike you very fast, over and over again. You must try to block all his strikes, as this helps you to hone your reflexes. Also, sparring is an excellent way to build up stamina and it gives you the chance to constantly test and improve your skills. I can never stress enough how important it is to work with the Chi Sao and the Hubud drill.

There are also many sticky hand forms from the Wing Chun and Filipino systems which can really enhance your reflexes to a very highly tuned level. Ultimately, at the end of the day, the most important thing is to put everything that you learn into practice, and the only way to get better and better with your reactions and mobility is sparring, in a very controlled manner but utilizing all of your own God-given tools. And when you do spar, do it standing up, trying to concentrate your weight on the balls of your feet to add lightness and bounce. Keep your strongest side forward, because you want your best side nearest to the target, it's all about speed, anything you can do to make yourself hit your enemy faster should be done, so long as it does not compromise on power. We do this by putting our entire body behind the lead punch, using our hips and feet to make our lead as strong as a boxer's cross. Try to work on perfecting your balance.

Always try to fight standing up, especially for street confrontation. You never want to end up the one on the floor. Fighting for competitions is very different, but this book is not about competitions. In the streets it is your life that you could lose and not just some trophy or belt. I would choose life over any prize or title. That is more important to me, to know that my family and I are safe because of what I have learned and trained for. The simplest way I have of explaining this is to say that, as a person you are not imitating a style but you are being yourself: The "Human Style". Your training should enhance your abilities and exercise your weaknesses. Add to your own strength with natural weights. By this I mean using your own body weight. Building huge, body builder torsos will slow you down, and when men in particular get like this, in later life they can even develop saggy man boobs and appear to need a bra.

Some of the most effective ways to use your own body weight are as follows, with a recommended 20 reps of 3 sets for each:

Push-ups.
Try to start with 20 reps, or your personal best, and build up from there. Choose form over substance; 1 proper push-up is better than 5 bad ones...
... Start with your body parallel to the floor, feet balanced on toes, palms flat on theground and parallel to the shoulders. Hands should be slightly wider than shoulder width apart. Slowly lower yourself until your chin is almost touching the floor, keeping your back straight, look ahead as it is better for your spine.

Squats.
Feet should be slightly wider than hip width apart. With hands on hips bend your knees and dip down as low as you can, keeping your back straight. To add to the intensity, hold the squat for a few seconds.

Sit-ups.
Lying on your back with fingers on your temples, not holding your neck, keep your legs bent at the knees to protect your back and bring your head and body up towards your knees. As you do this, breathe out and

suck in your stomach muscles and pelvic floor to increase core strength.

Jumping squat-thrusts.
A challenging move that will improve your stamina very quickly; start in a push up position, pull both legs in and jump as high as you can, land into a squat and repeat. Land with knees slightly bent to cushion the joints.

Chain punching.
Starting with left arm extended straight in front of you: make a vertical fist, punch then follow through with the right fist and punch, over the top of the retreating left hand, bring fists back to your centre. Remember to pull the left back very forcefully and fast. Imagine a target's nose directly in front of you, really reach out, at the last moment bend the elbow slightly to protect the joint.

Isometrics for arms.
With barbell minus the weights, stand in a low squat (horse riding stance) and rest the metal bar on your outstretched forearms. Keep it midway between your elbows and wrists. Try to add light-moderate weights either side, push yourself. Try to hold the position for as long as possible, not letting your arms drop. Several sets of 20 seconds is good. When you finally put the bar down your arms will feel very light and fast. Then get a piece of rounded wood, like a broom handle, tie a string to the middle of it and suspend a medium weight to the string then using your hands roll it all the way up and then down again.

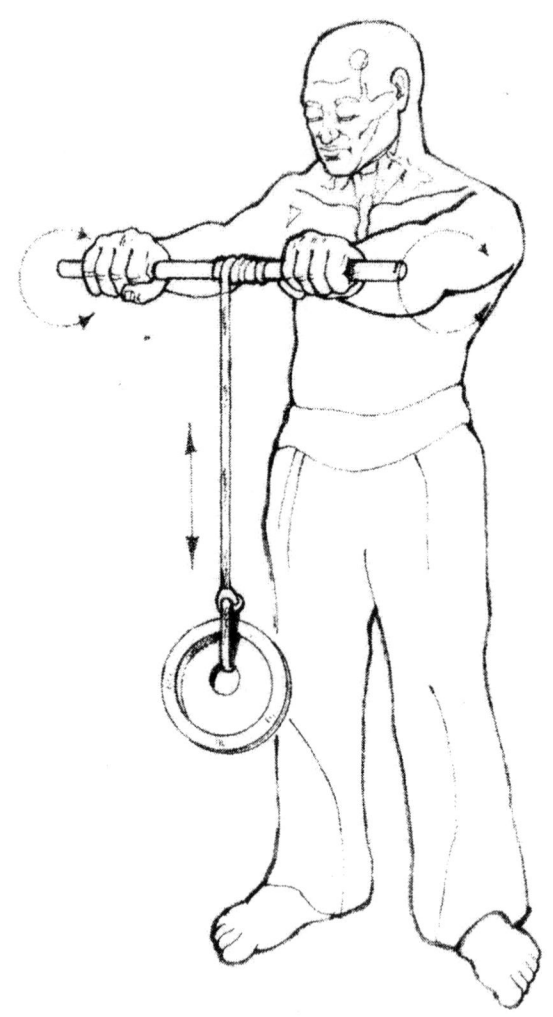

Do about 2 continuous minutes of this and your forearms will feel very solid. It is important to build up the strength in the forearms, so that they can be used as a shield to defend against weapons in a street scenario.

Bag work.
Try to get access to a punching bag. Most gyms have them. With bag work, you get a chance to work your stamina. Use various different palm strikes at your full force, as well as basic punches and kicks, also incorporate elbows and knees. Try to aim for several rounds of 3 minutes with a 1 minute rest between rounds. As your stamina improves, you should be aiming to get up to 15 minutes. Always warm up before your workout.

Blocking and striking.
When blocking and striking, try to do it very softly, almost like Tai Chi. Working on the technique is very important With your right leg forward (reverse if a lefty), lead with your left hand and with your left palm open, block outwards to your left side whilst punching with the right hand. Then parry inwards with the left hand and strike again with the right. From there, bring your left hand down, palm facing down and punch over the top, blocking a front kick to the midsection. Imagine you are blocking a punch that is coming towards you. Block and strike at the same time. Then imagine a roundhouse kick is coming towards you. Block down with the open palm of the left and punch with the right. Use a minimum of energy, always nice, relaxed and soft and the speed will come naturally. The next one is to block outwards with the left palm facing towards you face, elbow pointing down, and punch with the right hand. Finally raise the left palm above the head facing outward and punch out with the right. The palm upwards stops an attack from above. The purpose of repeating these exercises continually is to build muscle memory, so that in a street situation you will defend yourself naturally. You will not need to think, it should just happen. Keep thumbs tucked in on all blocks.

Sparring.
First and foremost when you are sparring you should be able to trust the person in front of you. When you are sparring, try to flow together.

Try not to bash each other's heads in because you won't learn anything from it, it will just be a test of egos. When you get close up and touch hands, work on the trapping. It is all about ebbs and flows. Don't rely only on your hands, but start to work the legs as well at the same time. Do your best to work on your mobility and footwork. Don't go to the ground if you can help it. When you put each other into locks, make sure you tap if it is painful or going too far. You want to finish the sparring feeling great, not injured. You don't want your veins to be bulging out, as your body should look natural. Go to a swimming pool as often as you can, move your arms and legs and do your exercises in the pool. The resistance is phenomenal and it really helps with building your explosive power. I like to practice the JKD form, as well as punches and kicks against the force of the water. It may look a little strange to the other people in the pool, but if you can kick effectively in water, you will kick amazingly in air. The boxer Mohammed Ali loved to train in the water, and his speed, power and agility were legendary.

Also, another good form of training without putting too much pressure on your own body is by strapping some light or medium weights to your ankles and walking around town. Walk up and down stairs this way as well, and stroll along the beach or by a river. Do not run whilst wearing ankle weights though as it deteriorates your joints. When you finally take those weights off you will feel like you can fly. Dancers often use this trick and you will find that your kicks will soon double, even triple in power.

Also practice punching whilst holding dumbbells in each hand. Do as many repetitions of the jab and cross from western boxing as you can, gradually progressing to heavier weights to build up your power and resistance. It is a good discipline to practice the various different blocks without a partner, to raise your own awareness. It is beneficial to stand in one place and practice blocking and striking at the same time. Repetitions of this will enhance your technique when you are working completely at your own pace. As for building energy, exercise can give you a lot more energy.

People who do not move about much tend to tire easily, but the more that you move, the more that you will be able to move. Move it or lose it is a very true saying when it comes to exercise. The benefits of regular, aerobic type exercises, when you get your heart rate up, can be pretty amazing. Feel good endorphins caused by aerobic exercise can counteract depression and leave you feeling confident and looking great too. Most important off all, you will be in a state of constant readiness for the time when being physical may be needed to save your life.

Try to keep your fitness levels up at all times. Try running, swimming, skipping, punching, bag work, anything and everything that is natural for the body, but never overdoing it, and resting between sessions. That way your body will never burn out. Also do your best to use the elements of the environment around you. Run on the pebbles of a beach if you live near one, as this makes your legs a lot stronger and more explosive for kicking. Try to run uphill as well. Even running up a slight gradient is much more effective than running on a flat surface. Also try to walk on the balls of your feet, as it gives that bit more of a bounce and adds the springy motion which will make your movements a lot more dynamic when fighting, and also in your training and everyday life.

Diet is another important factor in training. Eating in a balanced and healthy way, with lots of protein and wholemeal carbohydrates, fruits and vegetables pay off in the long run. Sugar should be avoided. It gives you a rush, which is followed by a slump in blood sugar. At this time your energy and reaction times will be under par, not good if that is the time you come under attack. Try to drink lots of water, especially when training. Dehydrated muscles perform under par. I also would avoid steroids like the plague. The appearance of big pumped up muscles can, and often does, hide bad health problems of people on steroids.

The following is a personal workout routine of mine. When doing this routine at first, give yourself a rest the next day or at least a couple times off a week. Allow your muscles to repair and renew their energy. Begin with some light stretching beforehand, but do not perform too much intense stretching before a workout routine, it is best saved for afterwards.

Basic warm-up routine:
• Jog on spot gently (1 minute)
• Bounce in boxing stance (2 minutes, sharply switch sides every 20 seconds or so)
• Circle hips (1 minute, change direction halfway)
• Star jumps (1 minute)
• Gently touch toes (30 seconds)
• Reach back, arch body gently (30 seconds)
• Finish here or repeat any of the above if desired until satisfied.

Basic unarmed combat training routine (30 – 90 second rest between exercises):
• 30 press ups
• 100 abdominal crunches (get yourself a yoga ball for best results)
• 50 squats
• Splits for 10 minutes
• Kicks (both legs): side 20 – front 20 – roundhouse 20 - back 20 - axe kick 20 - reverse 20
• Chain punching: 500 times rapidly
• Finger jab, hand over hand: 200 times rapidly
• Various power punches (both hands/10 each): straight punch - hook punch-back fist - upper cut - elbow strike - palm strike – power slap
• Shadow boxing, using all your tools and mixing it up (3 minutes soft – 3 minutes explosive)
• Finish with meditation, close your eyes and relax. Empty your mind and try to switch off from everything around you (refer to last chapter)

This is just a basic workout that I use. Try to train with it as often as you can. It should take between 45 minutes and an hour to finish. After a while you will see the impact and the difference that it will make to your ability. As you improve you may want to add some harder training, such as the training that I receive from my unarmed combat instructor, which I will outline further along in this chapter.

Remember to use your shield, which is your left hand, and your sword, which is your right hand (unless you are left handed in which case the reverse will be true), and balance is the most important tool of all. Your footwork must be properly grounded.

When attacked, you can use the finger jab to the eyes, palm strike to the chest, under the chin or under the nose. The power slap is a very effective and damaging blow, very good for striking in the temple, jaw or other parts of the head. But by far the best way to practice all these moves is to get yourself a punching mitt and kick shield, that way you can practise the techniques with your full force!

Get a partner to hold the pad/s, and in a single workout do 50 strikes of each of the techniques demonstrated in the following diagram on the next page (these include the knee, elbow, downward elbow, front kick to groin, and side kick). Also drill your palm strikes and power slaps on the pads as often as you can.

When it comes to the real thing, make sure you don't go straight into attack. You must defend before you attack. We never attack first. If your opponent blocks your attack, then you must flow into another defence and attack, each time countering his attack until you find an opening, and then you strike. My own unarmed combat training consists of applying those techniques described with a partner either holding a kick shield or pair of mitts. You can use the heavy bag alternatively though this is not as good training.

Here are some of my training tips, remember never to use your full power on your training partner unless they are adequately protected.

Alternative fighting techniques.
Try to be sneaky and use whatever works. The simplest move to take your opponent out could be a basic finger jab to the eye or front kick to the groin. Or there is a move which is even more painful than being kicked in the scrotum, and that is aiming for a front power kick into the lower intestines, which lie just below the navel.

Identifying vulnerable target areas.
These areas are the eyes, nose, jaw, throat and side of the throat. A palm strike to the chest will cave the chest in. Also to the solar plexus, lower intestines, knees or side of the thighs, which you can knee into to deaden the legs. There are various pressure points that are very vulnerable; a most effective point I have found is the one behind the ear at its base where the jawbone begins. Going for this area works 100% effectively, because the pain you will cause is unbearable.

Being on guard.
Well, the first thing is, never look at the ground. Always remember this, I know they say look your opponent in the eyes, but the most effective place to look is just under the throat. This way, you can really see the body moving and what shots he's going to throw in at you, peripheral vision is greatest here. Also you must react with 100% commitment.

Simple but effective techniques.
Simple ones are mostly the ones that will finish it with one blow. For example a side kick to the knee. Off and on moves are very dynamic and

explosive against any attack, whether it's a knife, gun or baseball bat, if you use the basic on and off principle you can't go wrong. Also use the elbows for very close quarter fighting and remember that trapping is a very important element, especially if you are fighting in a close- quarter environment. You are never going to be able to do a high kick in an elevator, so you use your hands, elbows, knees, head, etc. Also, I recommend using the figure-four locking. This is very effective and there are various different ways to apply the figure-four: two handed, one handed, with an elbow, in reverse, experiment on a partner to find what works and what doesn't. Always use what works for you, do it your way.

Momentum.

It depends on how you are attacked. You must use your opponent's energy against them. If there are two or even three to four attackers all at once, then the best thing to do is go up against a wall where you can be sure that no one is coming at you from behind. Always take out the guy who is making the most noise, or talking the most, then all the others should back off. If not, then be wise and keep your wits about you. All fighting comes from inside. It's an instinct that we all have. Sometimes you may even have an adrenaline rush and do amazing things like lifting a car up or grabbing a massive guy and throwing him across the room. But remember that adrenaline is a poison and any more than 30 seconds of it could kill you, so get the job done ASAP.

Combat mindset.

Well, for the combat mindset you need to meditate with some chilled out music. I usually use ambient music such as the sounds of dolphins or rain. This just relaxes the mind and makes you a lot calmer. I know a lot of people who go round saying; "I'm spiritual, I can do the Dim-Mak (Death touch), I'm spiritual, I talk to trees". I think that spirituality is a personal thing. It is like fighting or the martial arts in that you shouldn't go round bragging that you are this or that. What is important is how can you use this to make yourself and others around you better people, because that's what it's all about at the end of the day, the journey to your inner self. Training a calm mind benefits your balance, nerve, confidence, attitude, and overall ability to defend yourself effectively.

Sharp edged weapons/firearms.

During a knife attack you want to keep your hands up and tap away the knife with your left hand and your right, but the most important thing is balance before any defence. You can block the attack anyway you want to, but train to not expose your arteries too much. To practice this, mentally just split your body into four and then get your training partner to attack you towards the centre, to your right side, to your left and also a low strike. Use your forearms to protect against a slash to your face, or an attack from above. Your sparring partner should also try to push you against a wall with the knife against your neck. All your blocking moves against attacks should be practiced from the front and the back.

Guns are the same. A gun becomes useless when it's at close range and there are various techniques that you can use to disarm a gunman. It is all simple, to the point, and very effective. These techniques aren't taught in your everyday martial arts school and I don't teach them to everybody. I only teach people who have low confidence in themselves and legitimately want to be safe on the streets. I also try to help people who have already been a victim of an attack. This method is not about ego, it's about being true to the art of unarmed combat and with this in mind, the only time you should ever defend yourself with these deadly techniques is when you feel sure that your life is in danger.

Many of these I have explained already, such as the off and on techniques and simple strikes and blocks. The more advanced and effective methods can't be done justice on paper, I leave them to those who want to learn from me in person. Having said this, many of the reaction drills I have described here are excellent for this type of weapon scenario. Build your reactions and work on your balance and awareness using the methods I have provided in this manual and the techniques themselves will be the easy part.

Combat knife scenarios.

In this you work together in standing, kneeling, sitting and ground scenarios, staged as realistically as possible. As you become more proficient you can work with real knives. Try to overcome your fear of these weapons, so that in a real life situation they will not be so terrifying to you. You must always respect what damage they can do, but try to overcome your fear. Another great addition to training methods that I always recommend is those perennial favourites, the Nunchaku.

Nunchaku training is a very good way of warming up the hands, and the movements are very similar to blocking movements. Try to be fluid with them and don't do anything too fancy. Try to stick to the true principals.

If you are a beginner, get a plastic set with foam padding to save yourself from injury, when you get better switch to a wooden pair. Nunchakus are a great tool for coordination and for giving your hands explosive power and dynamism. Also remember that you should train with both your hands, don't just stick to your right hand but work the muscle memory on your left hand as well. The same thing applies to techniques. Never just work on your right hand. You should be able to work it with your left and right side at the same time or your fighting will always be restricted, and your whole arsenal in combat will be limited if you work only on your best side.

A good martial artist needs to be flexible. There is no point kicking if you cannot get your leg above waist height. If you can kick high, you need to be able to generate explosive power as well, not just high kick like a dancer. You have to have the power and the height connected, or it won't work. Go into the splits everyday and push your legs out as far as they can go and stay there for 5 - 10 minutes. You can also lie on your back with your legs up against a wall and then open them as wide as they will go. Once you have stretched, come up, give your legs a shake and then slowly go through each kick. Front kick, sidekick, hook kick crescent kick, axe kick; reverse turning kick, 360 degree turning kick. The following diagrams show you the exact dynamics of the 2 most important and useable JKD kicks, the side kick and round or turning kick.

1   2   3   4

If you have access to a Wing Chun wooden dummy it can add another dimension to your training. It is better to free-flow than to practice forms on it, you should be spontaneous, really drill your tools and use your imagination. When I train on the dummy I literally try to tear and bash the wooden arms off, go as hard as you can. See the diagram on the next page for some techniques you can drill on the dummy.

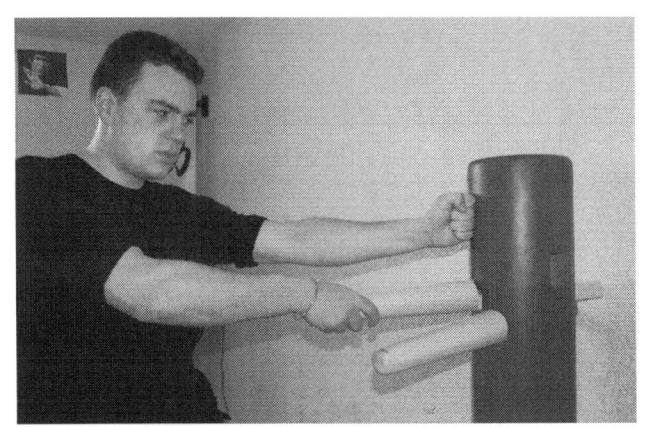

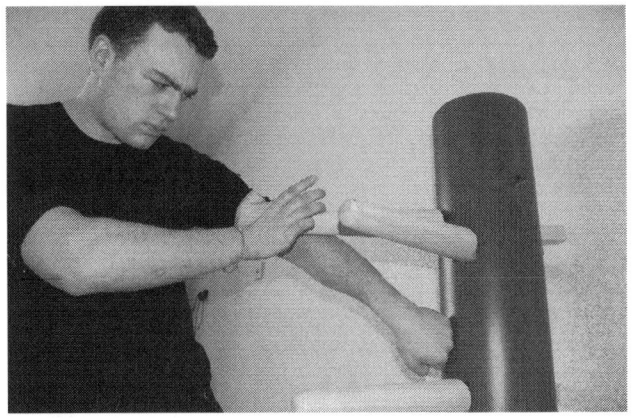

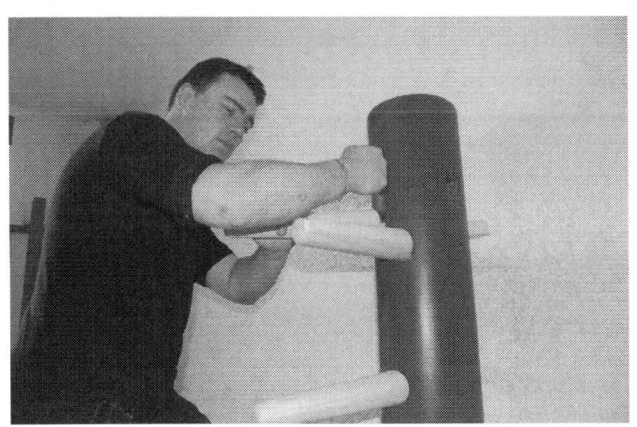

Once again though, I need to reiterate that there is nothing better than an actual sparring session. When you go up against another human being, only then can you apply your tools to their full potential. Do at least 12 rounds of 3 minutes each, and spar with someone that you can trust. Work on trapping combinations, kicking, locking and anything else that will work in a life threatening situation. Get your partner to attack you with a fake knife and see how well you defend yourself against it. This kind of role play training could save your life because it is reality based, and not any form of fancy trickery. When I am training I try to find the quickest and simplest way to take out an attacker in the moment of combat. Always aim for simplicity in your training. Remember, you have no time to go into a crane or a monkey stance; you must be quick and elusive like a snake. When training, remember that the highest state of martial arts is found in turning a technique into a formless state.

Chapter 6
"The true formula of Martial Arts"

"Life revolves around the Yin and Yang."

The yin yang symbol is thousands of years old. It was first developed by Chinese scholars as a way to observe the sun's movement and to understand the universe. They measured the length of shadows cast by the sun by putting a pole in the ground. In this way they were able to chart the number of days in a year. The symbol comes from the dark and light areas represented by the movements of the sun and moon. Summer solstice is considered the birth of the yin cycle, and winter solstice is the birth of yang.

Yin
Yin is the black side of the symbol. It carries a white dot that symbolizes a small part of yang being in yin. In the world, dark would represent yin and light yang. Matter is considered yin and spirit is yang.

Yang
The white side of the symbol is yang. Yang is the polar opposite of yin. Heaven and all things on the spiritual plane such as the soul are considered yang; whereas, the polar opposite is the material world or yin.

Cyclical
Yin and yang opposites are represented in the symbol as being cyclical. In the symbol, just as the white or yang side reaches it's highest point, or thickest part of the white, the yin begins. The cycle repeats itself. Also, each polar opposite is inescapable from the other because it contains a "seed" of the other. The entire symbol represents harmony and balance.

Martial Arts training is a good and ethical routine for the mind and body and in turn the body and mind is always sending messages and accordingly it reacts. All we have to do is to look and listen to understand what it says that's personal to you. The most important message is that love is the source connecting all life. Light energy vibrates throughout the universe, and so that force should do the same through you. It is a tangible reality experienced by mystics and seers.

The Tao (Art) means living and applying it in the right way. Look ,learn, and express yourself in the way only 'you' would know how as its really tailored to your own personal desires; look around you, its all there in nature, its speaking to you, waiting for you to look, listen, hear, and feel. You must always strive for your own truths and know that you can look and learn from those who have lived before you; with age comes wisdom and more often than not, the older wiser ones can show us the way.

When you do martial arts it opens one up to the spiritual side. It makes you more sensitive and helps you to pick up on things a lot more quickly. We all have this kind of power within ourselves; the challenge is just finding it and tuning into it. Sometimes I just look into someone's eyes and I can feel what that person is feeling.

If you have a dream or ambition in life and you wish to fulfil it, then don't let anyone stand in your way. Imagine yourself reaching out to a star that you have chosen in this vast universe. There are no limits. You make the limits. Focus and work hard and you will reach your star one-day. Real success comes from within, once you conquer yourself that's when everything around you will become a lot clearer. I believe that JKD is a perfect circle as martial arts systems go; and now the time has come for us to take the magic beyond our spiritual realm.

It is important to have another inner or spiritual base to martial arts. You have to take notice and be aware of messages that are coming to you via strange ways or through friends unwittingly. The reason I say this is because many simply ignore or don't see or know the true way of life and creations ethics, which involve Martial Arts and its philosophy. For instance, I feel that it is possible that on a few special or chosen days of the year, a door opens and an endless source of power can help bring you some kind of help, meaning or lessons, find your true love, enhance your beauty and health...even allow you to live free from care! Yes, all that and even more. You can even tap into that energy unconsciously, it's a deep thing that can happen randomly or you can help enhance it in many different ways along the way.

This tremendous energy source is as old as the universe itself and, for thousands of years, people have called upon its powers to help change their destiny! Now it is your turn to do the same! Learn to look, feel, hear, listen and take on board what is given to you. Take it and use it to train and exercise...but also do the same with your mind thoughts and actions. We all should have the right and the ability to turn dreams into reality! I know that once you've learned how to use your instincts, actions, good thoughts and energy, you'll be able to get everything you've always desired including being the fine tuned martial artist that we may all strive to be?! It is essential to ensure that you are always studying, and learning as we progress in our arts; martial arts is a spiritual freedom from within.

While I meditate I try to really switch off my mind and listen to my soul, it can be very daunting at first but then again you can become more intuitive. Remember that everyone on this planet has his or her own path to follow; there is a reason for everything. In the end we look back and realise this was why certain things happened the way they did. There are also a lot of signs out there and you can learn to read them, it can help guide you through your life, just listen to your heart and you will never go wrong.

At times I talk deep about various things on many levels with other individuals who understand where I am coming from and are also on the the same spirital wavelength as me; at the end if the day its all about having a spiritual ethical base. One friend said to me, "are you religious?" "I said no, yet inner martial arts also has a spiritual base as in doing right and wrong as in ethics and morals". He said, "So do you think the spirit or mind has a play in your martial arts?" I said, "with traditions aside to me, yes, as I understand it, once the spirit and your thoughts and all of the martial arts you've learned merges back into creation, it is at one with creation, therefore it is eternal as is creation. Each time the creation sleeps and reawakens the spirits that entered into it before the slumber, it will be within it when it reawakens; that's why its important to always pass on a truth, an art, martial arts to another person who may take it on board, add to it and then carry it forth, it is like the Ying Yang cycle.

When the creation/universe begins its return back into the slumber state, any spirit which has not been incarnated into a body will be extinguished. Any spirit, which has had at least one physical life, will then follow its path of destiny to merge back into creation. Seemingly, this is replicated in nature; for example, when a mother tiger will give birth to cubs, some of the offspring will make it, and some of them will not. In giving birth, the mother is attempting to ensure the continued existence of the species. I think in a sense, the creation, as in martial arts is doing the same thing. By creating new spirit forms (martial arts forms) it is continually attempting to further its own existence.

The martial artist allows much time for all his action forms to learn and perfect themselves; to me it would be illogical for the creation to create spirit forms and then not give them the chance to obtain knowledge and wisdom which in turn increases its own knowledge and wisdom and therefore bores new actions and styles to carry on.

Essentialy, it is about tapping into the energy and using the energy to flow in and out. Enabling you to be able to hit or trap without even thinking; it becomes automatic, and will come from within. If you look around carefully, everyone in the universe is on his or her own personal journey and it's fascinating when you put the puzzle together and see how it truly works. A true martial artist is responsible and is caring and does his utmost to keep everyone from thinking that he is any kind of a threat.

Symbols are important in representing something. The ying-yang symbol in relation to martial arts and what it symbolises, has many interpretations of the same thing that can be read and researched about. From my 'own' personal thoughts and experiences; similar to the circle of the sun, moon, the spiral of energy etc, the outer circle represents the same as life's cycle, or from the begining to end, and end to beginning, meeting, ending, then round again into infinity; the aspired image is also a primal archetype symbol which can be found in the art of indigenous cultures all over the world including pre-historic cave art. You can find the spiral integrated into such symbols (creative-spiritual energy) and in cosmic electromagnetic life energy. A double spiral can be found. These synchronicities are significant. When one thinks about how a magnetic field spirals about the path of an electronic stream, it starts to make sense. When aiming to apply any action for example, a fighting/action, I visualise the symbol in my mind which in turn fires me up, thus producing and signalling to my brain, turning that into a movement/energy to enable me to apply the move; as a result my actions become faster/better, and improved upon. After doing this for years my mind is in autopilot and my body with training has been conditioned to that way, becoming what I am doing, in thought, as so it shall be in reality. So to me the ying-yang symbol is simply an image of focus, similarly as when using a lucky charm, crystal or talisman; the yin yang symbol acts as an aid to my inner strength and understanding. We must all find our own way and tools to help improve our personal martial arts journey.

Chapter 7
"Meditation"

"Life is not a competition my friend, it is a search for one's true self".

I truly believe that if you do not have the right mindset, you will never grasp the true essence of Martial Arts. You have to not only transform your whole body into a weapon but must also tune your mind as well, so that it becomes at one with everything. Meditation is a great help in the control of anger, and in a fight or self-defence situation, getting angry is the last thing you need. Uncontrolled anger can be very damaging; it can make you forget and impede your performance of all of your well practiced moves and techniques.

This chapter will give you a basic outline of how you can begin to meditate, so that you can calm your inner spirit and tune into yourself, thereby finding out the true essence of what you are all about. To adapt oneself to any situation and, as Bruce Lee put it, "Be water, my friend", is the ultimate goal of the true martial artist. For this reason I feel it is imperative to train not just the body, but also the mind. In fact, training the mind is probably even more important than training the body in the long run.

Confidence and awareness are valuable tools. For anyone unaccustomed to doing this, the concept may seem strange at first, but to achieve true self-awareness one needs to let go of self-consciousness and embarrassment and just go with the flow. Meditation is a very good tool for looking inside yourself and your mind's central core. It's a way of tuning in and listening to your inner spirit. It can be difficult to explain what this all means, but once you begin practicing you will no doubt understand where I am coming from and the power involved.

Meditation can help your breathing and also keep you a lot calmer if you are attacked, so that you can take care of the situation without stressing out or losing control. Meditation, if developed properly, will give you a lot more awareness of your energy centers, and therefore make a huge improvement to your martial arts training.

There are many forms of meditation and the right way or wrong way is not set in stone. The art is in choosing one that suits you. Once again, focus on the methods that work for you. I have found that the most effective way is to simply find a comfortable place, somewhere that is quiet and peaceful. Sitting comfortably: close your eyes and relax your body and mind, remove stiffness, relieve tension from your shoulders, become weightless. Try not to think of anything specific; leave your mind empty. Of course thoughts will come into your head.

For anyone who is new to meditation or even those who have been practising for longer, it is practically impossible to completely block out all thoughts; acknowledge these thoughts as they come into your head, and then let them go. Do not try or work to push thoughts out of your head, simply ignore them, do not become distressed should they linger and they will go. This is the way we meditate after a hard workout, or a session of deep contemplation with ourselves (personal or intellectual), we forget about everything we've done or thought about and everything we are going to do or think on. We simply lose ourselves in the shapeless present and do not dilute this state with our worries, emotions or thoughts. Again, the best way to remove the random thought popping into your head is to ignore it, don't acknowledge the thought, accept it for the moment it is there then let it go, relax and it will happen by itself. At least 10 minutes is recommended for best results, but as you become more accustomed to your style of meditating you can work up to an hour or even more at a time.

Alternatively, an easier approach is to focus on an image in your mind, such as a peaceful stream, or a beach, in fact any place where you feel relaxed and safe. In your mind's eye you can summon up the sounds of waves lapping on a beach, or even feel the sun's warmth above your head. Visualizing a flower can be a very effective aid to meditation. Some hardcore martial artists might find this a soft thing to do, but it is invaluable for strengthening the mind in readiness for action. You can visualize the petals slowly opening. This type of visualized meditation is good for stress relief and teaches your mind to keep anger and negative thoughts in check. Once you become more used to entering the meditative state, you may not need these visualization aids.

Your whole focus should be on your breathing, but let it come naturally, breathe in through your nose and out through your mouth very gently. When you become more relaxed about meditation and breathing you can apply alternate nostril breathing. This is a very powerful method to clear the mind. With your right hand, close the left nostril with your middle finger, hold and gently breathe into the right nostril. Hold for a moment then release and breathe out through the same nostril then close the right nostril with your thumb and breathe in through the left nostril, and after a moment breathe out again through the left nostril. Continue this for a few minutes, using alternate nostrils and breathing very slowly and deeply, and as you become better work on holding each breath for slightly longer before exhaling.

When meditating in a calm state of mind, you should be able to hold your breath for at least a minute. If you cannot, practice regularly over time until you can simply by using a stopwatch or the clock on your wall. If you practice a couple of times each day you should better your time by 5 - 10 seconds every week. Once you can reach a minute, you can work up even further, 2 minutes is a fairly good standard. Do not keep your breath held if it becomes uncomfortable, that is counterproductive and dangerous.

Another dynamic way to apply meditation is to hold 2 medium weights, squat down into horse stance then hold the weights straight out in front of you. With your eyes closed, try to block out the fact that the weights are heavy and your arms are burning. This is a great test of mind over matter and you will improve over time if you practice regularly. I also find that the flowing, stylized movements used in Aikido can be a very effective tool for meditative awareness and calming the mind.

For meditation you can use whatever things that help you relax. Some ambient background music, a chanting CD, or a fragrant joss stick or candle, can all help you to enter that state of inner peace and harmony. A Tai Chi meditation technique is to stand in Mountain Pose. Feet hips width apart, arms by your side and hanging loosely, your hands relaxed and your back straight. With your eyes lightly closed, imagine a gentle warm rain falling over your body; try to feel the drops as they envelope you in warmth and softness. You can put your mind to the test by challenging the elements for real as well, perform a session of mountain pose outside by yourself the next time it rains, try to ignore the wetness and uncomfortable cold sensation, be as if there was no rain.

Meditating near the coast can aid your meditation as you feel the sea breeze against your skin. While you meditate try to forget about time and space; imagine that these things do not exist. I use meditation in every way, there are meditations that can help you increase your speed, timing, power, explosiveness, and especially the mind. Try not to think about mundane, everyday thoughts and problems. It is your thoughts that influence the flow of your energy.

Each time you meditate you go onto a different plane. Each time you close your eyes for at least 10 minutes, sit still and empty your mind, the exploration will take you onto a new level. It is a long journey. Just as with the physical side there are no short cuts, but if you take the long way, and really dedicate yourself to the true essence of what it is all about, then you will be learning and discovering many different things not only about martial arts but deep down within yourself.

Sometimes fear can prevent you from entering that deep state of relaxation. It is often a fear of the unknown. Some people even fear getting lost and never coming back. That won't happen. You will always return to the here and now, but as you learn to meditate deeply, you will enjoy staying in that state for longer periods. A trick that I have always found very useful is to close my eyes and visualize myself standing at the top of a very long stairway. The stairs can lead to any place you choose. I often choose a beach. I look down and see the sand and the hot sea and slowly start to descend the staircase. I try to feel the stairs beneath my feet and concentrate deeply on each step. As I slowly come nearer and nearer to the bottom of the staircase, I go deeper into the meditative state.

A good meditation tape or even a class will help you get over any lack of confidence that you may feel. It is a good idea to have a note pad with you, so that after each meditation you can note down how you felt, then go back to it later and see your progress. It is important to know how it feels to be in a meditative state. You can see your martial arts slowly improve and you will become more in-tune with your body and spirit. This is the most important aspect of martial arts. This is what a lot of people are missing out on. It is easy to punch and kick, but to have the right mindset, and to use that essence for a good purpose, is the main thing.

Martial arts are all to do with your mind and the more you concentrate your mind, the more you become in-tune with everything around you and also in-tune with your true self. Only then will you be able to express yourself honestly. In the end, martial arts, for me, are not about violence, and anyone who thinks that has completely missed the point. There is enough violence in this world.

Martial arts are about getting to know oneself. I don't care how hard or tough you think you are, because at the end of the day we all are fragile human beings and we all have insecurities about something. Martial arts are about conquering and fighting our own fears. The only justification that there can ever be for using violence against someone is when they turn their violence and aggression towards you or your loved ones first. Then you must do what needs to be done.

We must always strive to invite in the positive energies that are around us and release the negative energies from our being. I sincerely thank you for reading this very personal insight into my life and the martial arts principles I live by. I truly hope it has inspired you as an individual to follow your own path in life with confidence, conviction and integrity.

Please take the ingredients I offer and cook them yourself, mixing and spicing them as you think wisest. The road to truth in the martial arts and life never ends, but so long as we are being honest and faithful to ourselves, we will reach our destination and achieve our goals. My Urban JKD is a very personal expression of who I am, but I believe it can benefit anyone and everyone who is willing to consider its message. I could not have reached this point in my life alone, many great teachers and friends have helped pave the way here, and I thank all of them from the bottom of my heart, they know who they are. And to my students, those past, present and in the future to come, above all else... never stop training.

Best Wishes,
Emil Martirossian

Think on these things:

1. Try to be a good person, no matter how hard you have had it in life. When you are kind and respectful to all human beings and creatures and nature, you will get the same amount of love and respect back, if not more.

2. Everything that comes across as a negative you must turn into a positive.

3. Sometimes you feel your hopes and dreams are far away, what you don't realize is they are right in front of your eyes, ready to be grabbed.

4. Live your life the way that makes you content, so that when you look back on your past you will not have any regrets.

'Urban Combat, Jeet Kune Do' written by:
Emil Martirossian

Edited by:
Jennifer Gibson

Original sketches and illustrations by:
David Hemblade

Photographs by:
Jason Bayney & Howard Bland

Book Cover & Layout designed by:
Christine Lee
www.zen-design.co.uk

www.emilmartialarts.co.uk

Made in the USA
Charleston, SC
02 June 2012